A Race Divided

J. Oscar Bass, PhD

authorHOUSE™

1663 LIBERTY DRIVE, SUITE 200
BLOOMINGTON, INDIANA 47403
(800) 839-8640
WWW.AUTHORHOUSE.COM

First published by AuthorHouse 09/28/04

ISBN: 1-4208-0206-2 (sc)

Printed in the United States of America
Bloomington, Indiana

This book is printed on acid-free paper.

Printed in Bangkok, Thailand
First Printing, 1999
Second Printing, 2003

I dedicate this book to my youngest grandson, Allen Joseph Robert Coleman, born August 1999, with the hope that by the time he is able to read it, there will be more unity within the African-American race. With the further hope that by the time he is old enough to make a difference, he may find within these pages the encouragement needed for him to join with others in seeking to bring creative change within the world in which he lives.

– ACKNOWLEDGEMENTS –

I wish to thank a number of kind and dear people who have made this small treatise possible. For my wife and two daughters, who have never ceased to encourage me during the periods when I was living with some of the incidents about which I write and during the writing as well. We have grown a lot closer together as a family through this effort. Barbara Hooks, my untiring typist who had to endure the arduous task of trying to unravel my dictation and set it to print in a way that I could better understand what I thought I had said, is due a debt of gratitude that I can never repay. Thank you, will not even begin to express my sincere appreciation to Darlene Anderson who worked so diligently editing this work while at the same time proofing and editing my autobiography. Without her most pleasant attitude and journalistic abilities, this work would have never seen the light of day. She literally worked on this project until hours before it went to press. Thank you again, Mrs. Anderson.

Cookie, you have always been there for me during this and the six prior projects, and you've promised to stay by my side as the next project is launched. I have no words to offer that would be adequate for such a loving and supportive wife. Until the words come, let's just keep doing it together in the way that has brought us so much joy over the years as best friends and partners in marriage.

TABLE OF CONTENTS

Continued on next page

Introduction

After the departure of Rabbi Richard Levine of Temple Emanuel, which ended the Jewish religious presence in Willingboro, I became the senior religious leader in the township, with thirty years of residency. I was already the senior African-American pastor in the township, having founded the Alpha Baptist Church of Christ Nurturing Center in 1977.

Prior to the establishment of the Alpha Church, I was an executive with the American Baptist Churches and later with the Progressive Baptist Convention, two national Baptist denominations with long histories of demonstrated support of social justice, including the ministry of Dr. Martin Luther King Jr., who was affiliated with both groups. Therefore, I felt at liberty to become involved in the justice issues of my choice without any fear of objections from either of the denominations for whom I worked.

As I was a social scientist, pastor, and participant observer in the affairs of Willingboro, where I lived, my opinion on a variety of issues involving Willingboro appeared frequently in the Letters to the Editor on the editorial page of the *Burlington County Times.* Shortly after each letter appeared in print, I would begin receiving telephone calls regarding what I had written, and in many instances, others would write a letter to the editor referencing points that I had made in my letter.

It was through this medium that many people heard about me and developed some idea of my philosophy of justice, and on a number of occasions different people contacted me requesting my opinion or involvement in some justice issue they were facing. Although this was not the purpose for my letters to the editor, I was not disappointed that this window had been opened for me to be of possible assistance to people who were involved in the same or similar issue about which I was writing. In fact, I became so busy with responding to requests for help that I pulled back on writing letters to the editor. Therefore, I was not surprised when a member of my church called to make an appointment with me to discuss an issue of concern to her. On the day of the appointment, she arrived with a white woman who was also an elected official. They had come to see me, as I was one of the persons in Willingboro known to be interested in the public education system of the township. The two women primarily wanted an objective opinion regarding some concerns they had related to the way the political game is played in Willingboro on the school board and in the Democratic Party. They felt that they could talk to me because I had never been known to exhibit a blind loyalty to any particular party or candidate. Instead, my reputation over the years has positioned me as a known seeker for justice without regard to race, gender, religion, or political persuasion

During the time that we were in dialogue, a number of subjects were raised for discussion. Two stand out among the rest and are germane to this story.

One, the day of so-called clean elections, where a candidate ran for office fully independent of any outside influence, has probably passed for all elected officials. More specifically, it takes money to get elected to any public office in Willingboro today, and much of that money comes from the political party backing the candidate. In Willingboro, the Democratic Party is the party of choice for the majority of the party-aligned voters. Therefore, unless a candidate is running as an incumbent, it is the Democratic Party that puts up much of the funds needed for the campaign, and the influence goes with the money.

The women indicated that the Democratic Party has an interest in all elections, including the election of members to the Willingboro Board of Education, and that the party was not above putting "street money" in the hands of selected candidates to help assure their election. Street money represents funds given to candidates directly or to others working on behalf of the candidates on an as-needed basis. They knew that none of the conversations we were having was news for me; rather, it was a lead-in to the main reason that they had come to my office. They wanted me to offer a suggestion regarding how to bring about a sense of equity and harmony to the alignment of power during the reorganization meeting of a specific group to avoid a major conflict that could have a long-range impact. We discussed some ideas and settled on some that we thought were workable and beneficial to all.

As we were preparing to bring closure to the meeting, one of the persons casually opened another subject area that was not planned but proved to be the most important subject of all, as far as I was concerned. It was stated that just a short while earlier, a high profile person within the Democratic Party had made the observation that she had been selected to her position precisely for the purpose of keeping the African-Americans in line. According to this high-profile person, the African-Americans were really dumb people when it came to power because they had the strongest power base in the township but did not know how to harness it and use it collectively to their advantage because they were so divided among themselves. Thus, by default, this division among them created the environment that co-opted the would-be African-American leaders as pawns in the Democratic Party, while at the same time holding the remainder of the black population in check by not providing an issue for them to tackle. I was told that this observation was first made to the persons who were in my office and then expanded on, a week or so later, before a room of nineteen people. They said that everyone in the room was stunned but did not seem to know what to do about it. I told them I was not happy with what I was hearing and was not sure what I would do about it, but I was certain that what had been shared would not be erased from my memory.

I shared what I had heard with some of my colleagues at the clergy association meeting, and all were shocked to hear it, although one clergy person was familiar with the woman who had allegedly made the statements and felt that she should be challenged. We never made an official follow-up as a clergy group.

Looking back at the not-so-frequent attempts by African-Americans to be successful business people in Willingboro, individually and corporately, I see a picture that is not so pretty. In fact, I have to admit that the mystery lady referenced above was correct, although a bit bold, in making the observation publicly. African-Americans could and should have made more progress than they have, both economically and politically, especially during the past thirty years when their numbers began to swell in the township. This lack of significant impact on the part of African-Americans in the total scheme of things in Willingboro can be attributed in large measure to the division among them, which plays into the philosophy of Abraham Levitt, the developer of the town who did not want blacks as residents in the first place.

What have we learned over the past twenty to thirty years? Can things be better? Will they be better? I invite the reader to take a brief look at this through my eyes. This is not meant to be a scientific treatise, nor should it be construed as an exhaustive coverage of everything that has been associated with the African-American in Willingboro. Rather, it is an introduction to what I hope will be a much larger study undertaken by me or someone else in the not-too-distant future. One or two earlier efforts by African-Americans to mount political power will not be covered in this short chronicle because they disappeared from the scene without leaving any recognizable evidence of their existence except in the memory of a few older persons in town.

I begin by stepping back in time to 1958 to examine how the African-Americans came to live in Willingboro. From there, I will share some of the earlier observations that were made regarding some of the issues facing the community, and who some of the earlier players were. No attempt will be made to deny or shield my involvement in the attempts to further the cause of justice or minority economic development because I was a key player in what little was accomplished or attempted and failed. In some instances where African-Americans have or had a semblance of recognizable power, they did not earn it by coming up through the ranks, and therefore there is little history associated with it and it will be presented as such. In other instances, the white power brokers did not want to share any power with African-Americans and did not do so because the African-Americans did not have a united group behind them to demand justice, and this will be highlighted as well. I will touch upon the political structure of Willingboro so the reader can gain a better feel for how things work in Willingboro in that arena, and also why they work and why they sometimes don't work.

These are a few of the subjects that will be raised in this study. If some sound like mere fragments, that is the way they actually are at this point. During the gathering of information for this chronicle, I interviewed a number of stakeholders, did participation observations, designed and circulated questionnaires, and conducted interviews.

There was one major disappointment in the data gathering process, however, and it is related to the banking industry. They refused to return the questionnaires, although I submitted at least two requests and talked to bank officials. In every instance, they understood that I was conducting legitimate research as a legitimate research scientist and that all of the information questioned was required by law to be kept in the public domain. It is my belief that the banks are not too proud for the public to have demographic and other statistical data regarding their institutions in this regard. However, they are sending a strong message to that effect by not cooperating with my request, even though I was personally promised full cooperation by senior officials in two of the four institutions I contacted.

In the concluding chapter, dealing with the government of Willingboro, I will offer some suggestions as to where I think we ought to go from here as a community.

Our Town ~ Their Town

A Brief History of Willingboro
(Also known as Levittown, New Jersey)

WILLINGBORO is a residential community consisting of approximately 40,000 residents and 11,000 single-family dwellings, and comprising about 4,000 acres or 7 square miles of land nestled along New Jersey Highway Route 130. It is 15 miles south of Trenton, the state capital, 14 miles north of Camden, the state's poorest city, 17 miles northeast of Philadelphia, one of the nation's ten largest cities, and 65 miles west of Atlantic City, the East Coast Las Vegas. It is a township with a well-orchestrated, documented, and emotionally mixed heritage and a troubled, problematic, and uncertain future. It is a prime candidate for any ambitious student looking for a subject for a doctoral thesis. Within its narrow boundaries is a story that is most unique, but has never been fully told, especially regarding the African-American presence, the first minority group to take up residence in the township.

My focus is not geared as much toward setting the record straight regarding the African-American presence and their contribution to the development of Willingboro as it is to open a window through which their presence can be seen more clearly. My hope is that, in so doing, the prospects for their future may be more positive than in the past.

Since the arrival of the first African-American family in Willingboro was not by advertisement of the developer, invitation of the township, or the initiative of realtors, it seems most appropriate to give a brief history of Willingboro as perceived by its developers.

Willingboro was designed by its builders, Abraham Levitt and Sons, over a period spanning slightly over a decade (1958-1970). Speaking on the eve of its grand public opening for occupancy in 1958, William Levitt, the older of Abraham Levitt's sons, referred to the new Levittown as the perfect town in every respect. It was the dream come true for the nation's largest builder and developer, Levitt and Sons.

According to Levitt, there were seven features built into the basic concept and design of the town that would make Willingboro the most unique town anywhere in America.

Levitt was very careful to emphasize the newness of the Levittown, New Jersey, project, as it was decidedly different from, and better than, the projects the firm had developed in Levittown, Long Island, and Levittown, Pennsylvania. Although these earlier projects were financially successful for both the builders and the buyers, they were admittedly not ecstatic successes. This new Levittown was touted as having incorporated the best of the former projects but far exceeding them with new innovations both in design and structure.

The pride and pomp of the builder regarding the new Levittown, as outlined in the press release, can best be captured by reproducing the exact words that William J. Levitt used when announcing to the nation the grand opening of this historic community.

There are seven basic reasons why our new Levittown will be different and better than anything ever attempted by us or anyone else in the field of community building.

1. It provides for a school system planned and built in advance–and without the staggering load of public debt that cripples so many communities today.

2. It is one township and will be a municipal entity. The residents will elect their own government and run their own affairs.

3. We function under one set of ground rules, which means we can plan better and work cheaper. Trying to operate with four separate town boards and four separate school boards as we did in Pennsylvania, where we straddled four municipalities, was like trying to work a jigsaw puzzle with tied hands. [The reference is to Levittown, Pennsylvania, a Levitt project just across the river in Pennsylvania a few miles northwest of Willingboro.]

4. Precise planning for public facilities can be done in advance, because there will be a responsible public body to take over and operate the public facilities as they are built.

5. We perfected our concept of neighborhood planning. School, civic, and recreation facilities will be built exactly where they ought to be in centrally located park areas serving each separate neighborhood.

6. The houses themselves are the best we ever produced in value and appearance.

7. We are ending, once and for all, the old bugaboo of uniformity. Up to now we grouped our houses according to price, building the same basic house over and over again in the same section. To use a Detroit analogy, we put Fords in one place, Buicks in another. In the new Levittown, we built all the different houses, of different size, price, and appearance, right next to each other within the same section.

To sum it up, Levittown, NJ, represents an improvement over the past and will be a better place to live because our planning has solved many of the basic problems of towns and cities in the nation today–how it educates its children, how its people take a hand in local doings, how they spend their leisure time, and what the town looks like. (*BCT*-958)

However, arriving at the point where he could declare the new Levittown a success story in the building industry was not a simple matter and would have been almost impossible if the name of the builders were not Abraham Levitt and Sons.

Although Levitt was the nation's largest builder of residential housing, the company needed government-backed loans to ensure that young soldiers and members of the middle and poor classes could afford to buy one of Abraham Levitt's houses. Adding a bit of panache to his comments, he suggested that any one of the new homes in this project was comparable to any house in the suburbs purchased by members of the upper middle class a generation or more earlier.

The best part of all was that the present house purchase, although made decades later, was even cheaper now. There was one other very essential difference: unlike the large sum of money needed as a down payment to purchase an expensive house in a more traditional suburb, one of Levitt's houses could be purchased for as little as $100 down and $89 a month, including taxes. The purchase price was where Levitt could really boast. His new homes were priced between $11,000 and $14,000.

Levitt could afford to sell his houses in this price range because of a number of factors under his control. His houses were mass-produced, thus eliminating the need for a multitude of designs. Levitt and Sons had their own lumber company and made their own cement blocks and nails – the basic items for any frame building. Other items were purchased in bulk, thus benefiting from price cuts that were associated with extra-large purchases. Experience had also been a great teacher for Levitt. They had not only learned how to eliminate waste by not buying unneeded items, they had also precut and special packaged the exact quantity of each item that was needed according to the design of the particular property. Those items would be ready and waiting in a preformatted manner at each site, according to the needs of each specialist working on a given property.

Since there were no building codes that had to be followed, Levitt could trim the cost even further where possible. For example, Levitt wired the homes with insulated lead wire, which was cheaper than copper wire. In the structures, some studs were set wider apart than the 16-inch on-center, which later became the New Jersey Building Code standard. He often used a low-grade sewage pipe instead of PVC, which was an industry standard. Even on the front of the houses, he used a composition paper material for the fascia and overhang instead of real wood and composite plywood. Of course, by painting the composition paper with fresh coats of exterior latex satin paint, the anxious home buyer never knew the difference. It was not until a repair became necessary that the discovery would be made, and that would come long after any guarantee that came with the house had expired.

Another area of profit came with the poor landscaping that Levitt provided, which was little more than weed seeds (if there is such a thing). He did not provide sod, which normally goes along with a new house. At the very least he should have provided adequate landscaping service until the grass came up and was ready for the initial trimming. By not providing any of this, his profits were even greater. Levitt sold the house and the ground and made out well financially.

One year prior to the development of Levittown, New Jersey, William J. Levitt had testified before the United States Congress that the housing shortage had reached crisis proportions. He stated that the building industry was virtually at a standstill due primarily to the fact that the country as a whole was facing a general economic collapse, which was sure to worsen by the following year.

Even before the postwar crisis came with all of its impact, the building industry had indeed encountered the strain of tight money, which impeded the building of new homes at a time when they were needed the most by the blue-collar workforce. Levitt argued that although the government had demonstrated an interest in this regard, it should go much further and do much more by opening up more opportunities of credit to borrowers. This was especially important if there was to be an increase in the number of new housing starts and if the government hoped to help lessen the blow of the economic crisis, which impacted the housing industry.

Levitt was correct. The economic crisis came on schedule one year later, and the government's response to the crisis was both swift and positive. The channels to government credit were opened wider and the application process made easier, as Levitt had suggested.

Levitt's response to this new flow of cash was that he would build mass-production homes of higher quality and greater value. He put forth the idea to the general public that the best answer to an economic crisis was to release their limited resources and face up to the crisis by investing personal funds into commodities of high quality and value, such as a new Levitt home.

By pursuing this avenue, Levitt suggested that any recession would be held at bay and new jobs would be provided that would spark economic growth.

In the meantime, the Levitt firm, through representatives, began to buy small blocks of land in different sections of Willingboro, which at that time included parts of the borough of Rancocas. It wasn't until the firm had purchased a large number of blocks of property that the people in the community realized what was being planned for that vast area of farmland that contained only a few dozen houses.

However, there was a wrinkle in Levitt's grand design to build all 15,000 homes within a single township. It did not bother them too much that there were a few landowners, like Chris Stuart, who would not sell all the land they owned to Levitt. What did trouble Levitt was that 450 acres of land that Levitt needed was located in the Burlington Township, and two-thirds of the land area of Rancocas was in Willingboro.

The acquisition of the land Levitt needed within the Burlington Township was relatively easy; Levitt simply purchased it outright and later redrew the boundaries. However, the citizens of Rancocas fought to keep their residences as part of Willingboro Township. They had good reason to fight, as there was no monetary gain for them under Levitt's plan. Even more important, they would lose a part of their historic heritage if the boundaries were redrawn in such a way that they would lose their identity with Willingboro and become a part of Westhampton Township.

Thus, when public meetings were held around the issue, Rancocas citizens turned out in large numbers to protest. They argued that Rancocas was a well-established historic village founded many years earlier by the Quakers, and they wanted to keep their identity. If Levitt were permitted to have the boundaries redrawn, it would constitute the moral equivalence of throwing them out of their homes. By every count, they put forth a good argument and, perhaps, would have won had they been doing battle with anyone other than Levitt and Sons.

This was not the only hurdle that Levitt had to overcome before his plan to build 15,000 Levitt homes could become a reality.

By this time, William J. Levitt had become the president of Levitt and Sons and was very visible in all the key places in the township, county, and state. His visibility and money enabled him to win a lot of friends and buy a lot of power, and Levitt used both to the advantage of the Levitt firm. This was evident in 1956 when the New Jersey State Legislature passed two bills into law that directly benefited the Levitt project. Together those pieces of legislation made the Levitt development a single political entity. Although this action did not rest well with the citizens of Rancocas, it was touted as a blessing for the future residents of the new development and even beneficial to Rancocas, although the specifics as to how were not given.

The benefits to citizens of the new Levittown, however, were real. Instead of the residents having to deal with more than one municipality, as was the case in Levittown, Pennsylvania, in matters such as water connections, trash removal, and sewage disposal, the citizens of the new Levittown would only have to deal with a single municipal authority, which was precisely what Levitt wanted.

With this hurdle behind them, the construction crews began their work in accordance with the architectural and site development drawings that had already been completed and were ready for implementation.

Shortly after construction had begun, Levitt crossed another hurdle by getting the Willingboro Township to officially change its name to Levittown so that the general Levittown theme could be sounded in a third state on the Eastern Seaboard. This passed in 1959 by a close vote of 961 for the change and 881 against it. However, as the township grew and people felt more comfortable with their home purchases, the subject of the name came up again in 1962. This time the vote was 3,123 to change it back to Willingboro, with 3,003 voting to leave it as Levittown in deference to the developer. This was only the second battle that Levitt had lost, and then only by a slim margin of 120 votes.

That was forty years ago and since then Willingboro's early history has been chronicled and published by two different writers from two distinct disciplines and, needless to say, two varying points of view.

The first book on Willingboro, written by sociologist Herbert J. Gans, was entitled *The Levittowners*. Gans composed his work while Willingboro was still under development and had the advantage of writing from the position of a participant observer.

For the opportunity to study a town during its initial stage of development and watch it take shape and gain a personality of its own, Gans actually became a Levittowner by buying a house in Levittown. With a very small down payment and an agreement to pay $89 a month, Gans took residence in a Cape Cod house in Somerset Park and began his study. Somerset Park was the first of eleven parks that Levitt had planned, and the same park into which Levitt welcomed its first families on Tuesday, October 15, 1958.

Willingboro at that time had a population of 501 residents, with fifty new families scheduled to arrive each week.

At the ribbon-cutting ceremony, William J. Levitt, president of Levitt and Sons, stated that the population of Willingboro should reach its maximum of 60,000 in six years. By comparison, it took Philadelphia a whole century to reach that number and New York City even longer.

Over a three-year period, Gans lived in Willingboro and studied its people in ways consistent with his role as a sociology professor at the University of Pennsylvania and with the research methods of sociologists.

His book is still the best work available on the people of Willingboro from a sociological point of view. There is much more that could be said about the development of Willingboro, but it would not add to the data contained in Gans' book, which is still available in most public libraries on the East Coast today. This mini-revisit to the earlier days of Levittown has been made for the benefit of those who may not have read Gans' work.

However, since Gans lived and wrote about a Willingboro that predated the arrival of the first African-American family, his premier work made a significant contribution to the body of sociological literature in general but not to the study of African-Americans in particular.

Carol Suplee, a former newspaper reporter for the *Burlington*

County Times and a freelance writer, wrote in the 1990's the second book about Willingboro using the format of a storyteller. Although it was an interesting work, it made no significant contribution to the understanding of the African-American presence in Willingboro.

Apart from the two works mentioned above, there was a third effort in this regard offered by Priscilla B. Anderson in 1985. Miss Anderson, a member of the Willingboro Township Council at the time, applied for and received a grant from the Afro-American Division of the New Jersey Historical Commission for the express purpose of penning a work regarding African-Americans in Willingboro, since no such effort had previously been undertaken.

She titled her fifty-page paper, *The History and Contribution of Black Americans to the Development of Willingboro*. There are five subtopics to Anderson's work, which include "Highlights of the Township's History," "Contemporary Willingboro," "The History of the Black Struggle to Move to Willingboro," "Life for Early Black Families," and "Contributions of Unique Black Individuals."

Anderson wrote more as a politician than a historian or a social scientist. Even so, her work would have been an excellent springboard for further research and investigation if it had been given wider circulation or made available to the general public. However, with so few people knowing about her efforts, it has had little or no impact upon the subject on which it was penned. Perhaps her grant did not allow for such distribution.

Apart from these three references, if one is to find other significant writings about Willingboro, he or she will have to turn to the various articles written by a number of reporters for newspapers of southern New Jersey and, more recently, the *Philadelphia Inquirer*. (*The Burlington County Times* is on microfilm in the county library.)

I spent weeks browsing through the microfilm and made little or no progress, since every newspaper had to be searched for a story dealing with the African-American presence in Willingboro. I concluded that there must be a better way to accomplish this, so I decided my primary source of external data for this presentation would be to use the questionnaire and interview process, along with a search of minutes of various action groups in the Willingboro and Burlington county libraries.

The secondary source of data was my own experience as an active minister in the Willingboro Township for thirty years, longer than any other minister in town and longer than most African-Americans have been living in Willingboro.

Additionally, I have been an active player, directly or indirectly, in much of the happenings relative to African-Americans in Willingboro and to a lesser degree throughout the county. This posture afforded me the unique opportunity to be able to speak empirically and objectively regarding the plight of the African-American sub-cultural group in Willingboro.

Thus, my single purpose in writing is to help bridge the information gap between the time that Abraham Levitt and Sons first crossed the Delaware River in 1954 with their dream of a new Levittown and today, 1999, when Willingboro is facing an uncertain and troubled future due to a number of factors. Perhaps the most important factor in the future of Willingboro is the African-American. Before turning to the nature of the African-American presence in Willingboro and in Burlington County and what that means for the future of Willingboro, it is important to revisit the story of how African-Americans came to be a part of Willingboro. I will discuss what they have accomplished, as well as their strengths and weaknesses. Then and only then can we look adequately at the prognosis for their future on the eve of the twenty-first century.

I will ask: What can African-Americans do to make Willingboro a town far better than even Levitt's dream, if that is possible?

Although I am a sociologist with a loyalty to factual knowledge, some liberties may be taken in this presentation due to the personal factors mentioned above. Having been personally involved in so much that impacted the African-Americans in Willingboro, especially in the religious and political sectors, I must take some liberty in order to present a side of the various incidents that comprise a significant portion of their tenure in the township.

Here a perception is referenced that perhaps would not and could not be told by anyone other than myself. Thus, to be silent is scary and to speak out boldly is risky. In the first instance, I could die before the next possible investigator came along with an interest strong enough to want to interview those whom he would identify as having information germane to the focus of this presentation. Even then, it is questionable whether or not other informed African-Americans would cooperate with any potential investigator out of fear of reprisals from those who are in positions to bring a negative impact upon them for publicizing that which was meant to remain unknown.

Telling the story of the African-American presence in Willingboro is also risky for myself because of possible reprisals, perhaps even more so because I am dealing with empirical attestation where others would be dealing with biographical data and third-party references.

And yet, as a sociologist and a man of the cloth there is really no other option but to tell the story as it is known to me for the benefit of the whole community of Willingboro, not just the African-Americans. Whatever the future holds for any of the residents of Willingboro must be available equally to all of its citizens or to none of them. And to that extent, all of the citizens must work together to bring about a future in which they can take individual and collective pride.

Now that the decision has been made to share the untold part of the Willingboro saga, the next decision has to do with where to begin.

Since the focus of the presentation is upon the impact of the African-American in the various spheres of Willingboro, the best place to begin is with their initial arrival in the township.

To accomplish this we must go back to the introductory paragraphs of this section and state more emphatically what was only casually implied. Without question or doubt it was never the intention of Abraham Levitt and Sons ever to have African-Americans as initial or potential residents of what was to be their dream town.

Selling homes to whites only had been both the policy and practice in the two previous communities that Levitt had developed, and Willingboro was not to be any different. Speaking on the issue, William Levitt was quoted as saying, "As a Jew, I have no room in my mind or heart for racial prejudice. But I have come to know that if we sell one house to a Negro family, then 90 to 95 percent of our white customers will not buy into that community. That is their attitude, not ours."

From this statement it is clear that Levitt was interested in the profit motive more than humanitarian issues. Being a Jew, he should have remembered with horror, and perhaps even anger, the prejudice that supported the Holocaust and cost the lives of six million Jews. That fact alone should have been reason enough for Levitt to have actually tested the climate in the proposed Levittown, New Jersey. Since the need for housing was so great, it may have been possible for Levittown to have been integrated from the outset, as it would have been difficult even for a white racist to resist the opportunity to own a quality new house so cheaply. At least Levitt could have raised the question as the alleged unbiased developer that he claimed to be.

The second question has to do with the matter of law. Levitt and Sons, while enjoying the prestige of being the nation's largest developer of residential housing, surely had a legal department or at minimum a staff attorney or one on a retainer. Why did Levitt not investigate the New Jersey statutes to see if there were any references to antiracial discrimination in housing as a matter of law in the state of New Jersey?

New Jersey did have a law on the books that prevented racial discrimination in housing. Although this law had not been tested, it was in place and would have been easily detected if the Levitt fine had raised the question. In reality, there was no evidence that Levitt's heart and mind were truly nondiscriminatory as previously claimed. Could it be that they knew about the New Jersey law but ignored it with the hope that African-Americans would not test the law? Or maybe Levitt intended to have all the properties sold before any potential test case surfaced and made its way through the courts. Although these questions may never be answered, the position taken by Levitt was just left of being stupid because at the time the whole country was in a rage over the race issue. There was no way that a project as large Levittown, New Jersey, could be built and occupied without a challenge sometime during the course of a decade or more, the time that would be needed to complete the building effort.

Integrationists, fueled by the landmark civil-rights case of 1954, were on the watch for areas to test existing civil-rights laws and to lay the groundwork for new ones.

Once again, the profit motive took precedence over the justice issue, and Levitt proceeded with the development of their all-white community, seemingly oblivious to the existing law against racial discrimination in housing. Or perhaps they were willing to face whatever potential hurdle they might encounter in the future.

Ready or not, the future came sooner than later. Levitt faced an otherwise suspended reality when Willie R. James, an officer in the United States military stationed at Fort Dix, and Franklin D. Todd, of Burlington, New Jersey, made attempts to purchase homes in Levittown, New Jersey. When they were denied the right to purchase, a decision based solely on the fact that they were African-American, they took Levitt to court.

This would have been a perfect time for Levitt and Sons to take the lead, not only in building new communities, but also in building human relations. Instead of taking a stand for justice and equality by vowing to uphold the laws of the state of New Jersey,

Levitt decided to fight back, although he knew that he was wrong and could not possibly win legally. Was this a business decision or a racist one? The reader will have to judge for himself. However, there are a number of factors that can aid the reader in the decision-making process.

It is not my position to force any decision upon the reader. However, it is my task to present as much of the facts as possible in every instance in order that the reader may come to conclusions based upon verifiable evidence.

To that end, an interview was conducted with one of the plaintiffs in the case against Levitt. A summary of that interview follows. Much of what is written here was also stated before the Willingboro Rotary Club in its February 1999 meeting.

Willie R. James stated that in 1958, two years prior to his retirement from the military as an army officer with a military occupational specialty in criminal investigation, he was stationed at Fort Dix, New Jersey. He was looking for a place to settle with his wife and family after retirement.

He looked in several areas around southern New Jersey for a suitable retirement home. In the process of that search, he heard about Willingboro and the new homes that were being built there. After investigating all of his options, he concluded that Willingboro offered the best of everything—the best house for the money, good schools, and a beautifully designed community. Therefore, he and his wife made the decision to buy a home in Willingboro. James reported that he talked to the people in the Levitt sales office and was told that houses were not going to be sold to blacks.

Not satisfied with that response, he went to Levitt directly and was personally informed by Levitt that blacks would be permitted to move into the town when it was all completed, but not while it was under construction. (By that time Levitt would be gone and any problem of racial integration, or the absence of the same, would be left for the township to resolve as Levitt went on to bigger and better projects.)

James said that a short time later he was informed of a new anti-discrimination law in New Jersey, and Levitt's denial of his right to purchase a home was in violation of that law. He was advised to file a complaint, against Levitt, with the Civil Rights Commission for racial discrimination in housing. This seemed easy enough since there was a whole bastion of lawyers willing to take the case pro bono. Before the case was settled out of court, nearly one hundred lawyers were vying for a piece of the action in this highly-publicized case.

Interest in the case seemed to be coming from all sides, including the office of the governor of the state, the office of the attorney general, the State National Association for the Advancement of Colored People, the American Civil Liberties Union, and the Civil Rights Commission. That is why so many lawyers were available to assist James with his complaint. Roy Wilkins, the national executive director of the NAACP and a highly respected African-American, also took an interest in the case and requested that James head up a local branch of the NAACP. James agreed to head the Burlington County NAACP. Individuals who were in the battle with James, fighting for human justice, were Rabbi Richard Levine of Temple Emanuel in Willingboro and Reverend Earl Tolbert of Second Baptist Church in Burlington, New Jersey.

The New Jersey attorney general told James that he would no doubt win his case, but he would probably never get a new home in Willingboro since the wheels of Justice turn extremely slow. By the time the legal battles were over, all of the houses would be sold or the price would be out of the range of his purchasing power.

Indeed, the lower court did rule against Levitt, and he appealed to the next level, and again the ruling was against Levitt. The case went to the State Supreme Court, which also ruled against Levitt.

In the interim, some unusual things began to happen in the career track of Officer James. Without any advance notice and for no apparent reason, he received orders from the base commander to go to Korea, which would have virtually ended his case. However, senators Clifford Case and Harrison Williams intervened and James did not have to leave the country. Staying in the fray and keeping the pressure on, Levitt gave rise to a second round of orders for James to go to Korea. Again, senators Case and Williams interceded and James did not go. Finally, the base commander gave James sixty days to get off the base and find residence somewhere else. Since this could not happen in Willingboro, it would most certainly have removed James from the fight, as he would already have housing. As if this were not scary enough, James subsequently received orders to be in California by the following Friday. Once again, the good senators intervened, leaving James to continue the fight for his right to purchase a home in the new Levittown. After this series of unusual happenings for the military, James received a call from the provost marshal, who told him that since James was a criminal investigator for the United States Army, there was no need for him to come to work because nothing was happening that required his presence. James related that he went in for 3 or 4 hours a day anyway.

What motivated the commanding officer of Fort Dix to have orders cut twice reassigning James to Korea and later issuing the order for him to move off the base? Who was behind it? These questions were never answered, if indeed they were ever asked. James believed that the powerful firm of Levitt and Sons was behind all three incidents. If James was correct in his thinking, and it sounds reasonable, then this offers more evidence that Levitt may not have been totally honest in his claim that there was no room for racial prejudice or discrimination in his heart and mind.

Levitt did not give up his legal battle to keep his new town all white until it became apparent that the United States Supreme Court was not going to hear the case on appeal. In essence, he simply lost. Whether he liked it or not, his new dream town now had, as a matter of law, an open-occupancy policy.

As a last resort, Levitt hired a husband and wife human-relations team to aid the town in making a peaceful transition from an all-white town to a limited integrated town. This team, along with other groups such as the Society of Friends and the NAACP, worked behind the scenes for five months preparing the white people in Willingboro for the arrival of a limited number of African-Americans.

Levitt, in conjunction with the realtors, had his salespeople and representatives go around to the various areas within the parks and ask the members of the white community if they would object to having a carefully selected African-American neighbor. If the homeowner said no, then that was where the African-American would be placed. This was a very evident case of racial steering, which apparently was not against the law.

This particular activity by Levitt seems to indicate that the white citizens were more concerned about the quality of life their new African-American neighbors would bring with them than they were with Levitt's need to be in compliance with the law. Levitt could have tried this latest tactic from the outset and even if the response had been negative there would have been more reason to sympathize with him as a businessman who happened to be Jewish.

Slowly African-Americans began to move into Levittown without any violence or even picketing, which would have been legal. Although other African-Americans were moving into Levittown on a selective basis, James was told that he could not buy a house in the new community as long as his case was pending. However, he did win a concession from Levitt: he would be able to buy a home at the original selling price when the case was over.

Actually this arrangement helped to bring an end to the whole legal battle, and James and his family moved into their new home in Milbrook Park in 1960, where they remained until 1974.

As if all of the prior action on the part of Levitt to keep Levittown as an all-white community were not sufficient to expose his double standards, he made two additional moves that spoke to this issue. First, he advised James to move his family into their house either during the day or very late in the evening rather than on a weekend to lessen the visibility of the family. James listened to Levitt but did just the opposite of what he suggested. He moved his family on the weekend during the hours when visibility was at its highest. There were no incidents, and although they received a few prank calls immediately after they moved in, those quickly ceased.

Levitt further proved that in his heart he was opposed to integration when he provided free land for white religious denominations to build their houses of worship. Levitt gave no thought to the religious needs of the African-Americans who would be living in the community, even if by force of law. But the impact of Levitt's decision not to provide free land to African-American denominations was further maligned because when he departed there was not a single piece of unimproved land in the township large enough for African-Americans to purchase and build their own houses of worship. In that respect, his prejudice against African-Americans hit them the hardest by virtually making it impossible for them to have their own houses of worship. In effect, Levitt was saying to the African-Americans, you may have won the right to live in this town, but not the right to worship here. In this later instance, there was no way to redress this particular prejudicial action as Levitt was not in violation of any legal statutes, although his actions were morally wrong.

As Levitt built his last Willingboro home and pulled up stakes and left the town of his dreams, one wonders what really went on inside the mind of one of the most powerful men in America. He spoke with a silver tongue but seemingly had a heart of stone.

As the leader of the county branch of the NAACP, James, along with others, observed that there was an absence of black presence in administrative positions throughout Burlington County. There were no blacks with key roles in the civic sectors, service areas such as department stores, or even stores on the Willingboro Plaza. They decided to picket those places that were not employing blacks. The loss of revenue from the black community caused many of those establishments to change their hiring policies.

In summary, the invasion of African-Americans into Willingboro was accomplished rather smoothly. During those early years of integration, there were riots in the schools and fights in the streets between black and white youth, but none of these were very serious and never rose to the level of adult involvement. However, the township did sense the need to establish a human-relations commission to help deal with these youthful encounters.

After leaving Willingboro, James moved to Rhode Island, where he became a pastor for thirteen years. Presently, James lives with his wife in their Edgewater Park home.

Even after going through a long and tedious battle for racial justice, James remains an intelligent, humble person without a thread of bitterness. It is ironic that Willingboro Township, which has named schools and streets in honor of many who have made much lesser contributions to the development of the municipality, saw no need to honor James, the man who was responsible for the integration of Willingboro. And yet, when the people of Rhode Island learned that James was a pastor in their state, they, through the leadership of the Urban League, gave James his first and only recognition for the contribution that he had made, not simply to Willingboro but to humankind as a whole.

The last point that James made in the interview bears quoting because it speaks at least indirectly to the latent racism that remains a part of our society: "The township officials accepted the racist attitude of Levitt, otherwise he would not have been able to get away with it as long as he did." This view and that of the religious experience of African-Americans will be revisited before this treatise is over.

Willingboro ~ A Future Place to Reside

TEN YEARS after Willie R. James had paved the way for other minorities to move into Willingboro, my wife, Charlene (Cookie), and I purchased a home in Willingboro.

We came to Willingboro from Bangkok, where we were serving in ministry, fresh from an experience, like James', of discovering, exposing, and eradicating discrimination in housing. This was ironic because the leaders of Bangkok did not even know that the problem existed until we encountered it purely by chance.

While in Bangkok, Cookie began suffering from an extreme case of shortness of breath due to hay fever. The doctor suggested that the problem would be helped or even alleviated if she slept in an air-conditioned room and spent much of her time under climate-controlled conditions. The only fully air-conditioned places to stay were apartments, of which there where plenty in the city. We decided to move. The question was, which apartment? Finally, we located a beautiful building, with a vacancy sign outside, near the international school.

We went over to the rental office, filled out an application, wrote a check for the first month's rent and security deposit, and indicated that we would start moving in the next day. The owner gave us a copy of the signed one-year lease, a receipt for payment, and two sets of keys.

However, the next day when we went back, the owner of the apartment building greeted us and asked if he could talk to me. First, he gave me a large envelope stuffed with a lot of Thai money. It was the Thai equivalent in baht (Thai currency) of the amount of the check that I had given him the day before. With his head turned slightly away from me, he said that we could not take the apartment. While offering the money back to him, I said that we had a signed lease for one year and that it was a legal document. I demanded to know why he was trying to get out of the deal.

With his head still turned away from me, the owner said that seven white American tenants had called him and told him that if he rented an apartment to a Negro, then they and all the other American tenants would move immediately.

I could not believe what I was hearing. Here I was, 10,000 miles away from America, in a country that had never experienced slavery as it was known in other parts of the world, that did not have a concept of actual racial prejudice and certainly not against the American Negro, and I was being discriminated against. The owner tried very hard to get me to understand that the reason for his refusal to let us stay in his complex was purely economics. He still owed a lot of money on the building, and if he lost his tenants, all of whom were white Americans, he would lose his building.

I could not let this rest. Utilizing my skills as a sociologist, I tried to put this whole experience into some kind of perspective before I took it any further. I had to do some research. So over a ten-month period I documented the existence of discrimination in housing in Bangkok, charted its extent, and examined its principal cause.

I was now fully armed with all the relevant data regarding the presence, extent, and cause of racial discrimination in housing in Bangkok, evidence that pointed to the white American, who had transported his prejudice from America to a country where he was a guest. I knew that I had to find a way to bring an end to this unfortunate practice without causing an economic loss to the Thai landlords or great embarrassment to the American government.

I decided it would be best that I go and talk to the American ambassador personally about the housing situation and share my data with him. The ambassador seemed glad to meet me and not at all happy that white Americans had introduced discrimination into Bangkok. He assured me that he would work with **me** in every way possible to bring justice to this situation without involving the Thai government or letting it reach any of the local media. In fact, he asked me to be in on all meetings that he would conduct with his diplomatic core and every person related to any aspect of the American Mission in Thailand. Frankly, this seemed like the best approach.

But in the meantime, his wife jumped ahead of us with her own version of a cure. In a special luncheon, with the queen of Thailand present, the ambassador's wife addressed the issue.

With fire in her eyes, she said, "I am speaking to all white women and especially to the American white women. I'm aware that Negroes are facing discrimination when they seek to rent an apartment because the white tenants threaten to move if the landlord rents to a Negro.

"Just to make sure that this situation is corrected today, I am insisting that you and your husbands pack in your suitcases the prejudices against Negroes that you brought with you to this country and leave them there. The ambassador will not tolerate any exercise of discrimination while you are on Thai soil. Therefore, before the day is over, you and your husbands go to your landlords and inform them that it is none of your business who becomes a tenant in their buildings and that it will not affect your own tenancy.

"If you feel that you cannot do this, then you should prepare to be on the next plane out of Bangkok tomorrow."

Within two days, the word had reached every landlord in my survey, and they said that they were now willing to rent to any Negro who qualified. We knew that it would take some time before we would be able to tell if the racial barrier had actually been removed. We set up a committee to hear cases of discrimination, and in a year they did not receive a single complaint.

We concluded that the problem had been resolved.

Not long after this, we returned to the United States from Bangkok on furlough. Upon my return, I was asked by some denominational executives to serve on the Interdenominational Crisis Intervention Team as the American Baptist representative for the remaining part of our year's furlough. That was in early August of 1968. By the time I gave my positive response to the request, I had learned of a Black Power Conference scheduled to be held in the Church of the Advocate in Philadelphia. I chose to register for and attend the conference, hoping to learn more about the crisis in America, since I was going to be on a team that traveled the nation helping to put out the flames of racial unrest, especially in areas where we had churches.

The experience at the conference was a rude awakening for me. Besides being held up before the group as a brother who had come back home to work in a struggle where he belonged, I was also rather jokingly put on the spot by the conference leader. The reason was that I had a slight Thai accent and could not say the word "black" the way *they* thought I should. Actually, I did not take it so much as a joke, as I had not been around a black audience of that magnitude in more than six years.

When the conference was over, I knew two things for sure: one, when I left America, people of my ethnic persuasion were called Negroes, and when I returned they were to be known as black. The country had changed. Martin Luther King, Jr., had been assassinated, and judging from the environment of that conference, the racial tension in America at the time was near volcanic proportion.

The second thing that had struck me hard was the fact that as a minister and a budding sociologist, there was no way I could go on another foreign assignment. I realized that I needed to apply my education and experience here in America. Equally important was my desire to complete the work on my Ph.D.

I requested and received a release from the Foreign Mission division of the denomination and took an executive position in the division of World Mission Support with the same denomination, which was an upwardly mobile move. This not only allowed my family and me to remain in America financially secure, but it also permitted me to continue my travels on a sustained basis to all the areas where we had churches. I was especially interested in visiting churches where a new face and voice might relieve tension.

The decision, however, to stay in this country presented us with the problem of where to live. Initially, we stayed in temporary housing in Philadelphia but decided that it was not the place we wanted to bring up our two daughters. We subsequently moved to the campus of Crozer Seminary in Upland, Pennsylvania, as missionaries in residence. This is the seminary where Dr. Martin Luther King, Jr., had received his theological education a couple of decades earlier. We were the first African-Americans to serve in residence on that campus. While there, we began our search in earnest for a permanent place to live.

The search ended when a fellow staff member and a former college buddy told us about the house that he had purchased in Willingboro. We went over to his house for dinner and he showed us the town. And, just as it was for Willie R. James, it was ideal for us in every respect.

We selected a house from the site map in Levitt's sales office. We were told that our home would be completed in about six months, and that it was the first house to be completed in that section of Garfield North. The selling price was $24,500. We put down $5,000 and signed a note for $136 a month. We moved in on schedule on August 10, 1969, and the second family to move to that section was also black and moved in August 11, 1969. The next several families that moved in were white, and my wife did for them what she had done for the African-American family: she took them some refreshments when they were midway through unloading their furniture.

Moving to Willingboro was truly a memorable experience, far different from what we had experienced before going into foreign service, and even different from Bangkok. We were now settled in the place where we would perhaps spend the rest of our lives. My wife interviewed for a teaching position at the Garfield East School in September of 1969 and was hired on the spot. She retired in 1997, having taught at the same school for twenty-eight years.

My new position with World Mission Support required me to travel 60 to 70 percent of the time, although I tried to be home on most weekends so I could worship with my family at the Parkway Baptist Church, where we had become members. There was a need for deacons at the church, so I accepted the role. It was the first and only time that I am aware of that an ordained black minister served as a deacon—a kind of self-induced demotion, which was unheard of in the black community. Had I not been an American Baptist in a predominantly white denomination, this would not have been possible.

It was while serving in the role of deacon under the leadership of a white pastor who was a bold and courageous fighter for racial justice that I felt the need to be involved in the local community as much as possible.

Since I had been a member of the Republican Party before going into foreign service, I declared my allegiance to that party during the next primary election. Being an African-American Republican was something of a novelty in Willingboro at the time. Willingboro was and still is a Democratic stronghold. Later I became a committeeman from my district and attended a few Republican Party functions.

The Willingboro Rotary Club

SINCE I HAD been a Rotarian in Thailand from 1965 to 1968 and had enjoyed the experience, it was not difficult for me to allow my name to be proposed for membership in the Willingboro Club in 1969. After being a guest of Robert Smyth, the pastor of St. Paul United Methodist Church, at two prior meetings, I was graciously accepted as the newest member of the club. I was entering the Rotary Club in America with great joy, not knowing that I would eventually leave with great sadness.

Although it was not mentioned at the time, my induction into the club also meant that the Willingboro Rotary Club would have its first black member.

As a member of the Rotary Club, I met perhaps all of the movers and shakers in Willingboro and established a good rapport with many of them, including but not limited to Frank Quinn, William Kearns, Edward Kelly, Marvin Ellis, Uri Taenzer, and John Tegley, to name a few.

To my satisfaction and for the benefit of the club, I immediately became a hard worker. My first project was building the Fourth of July parade float. By this time the second African-American, Harvey Beecham of Harvey's Bakery, had joined the club. He became my right-hand helper. I was also very involved in Give-a-Christmas, a program jointly sponsored by the Rotary Club and the *Burlington County Times*. I initiated the idea of investigating the people who made requests for donations to see if the claims of need were legitimate. The house for battered women, now known as Providence House, was another Rotary project that I strongly supported. I was also community service director for Rotary.

Our club was the first in the district to come out very strongly in favor of an open membership that would allow women to join. I, along with Frank Quinn, then president and the most influential member of the club, led the vote in our club to include women. The vote carried overwhelmingly but did not have the weight of law, as Rotary International had not as yet adopted an open membership policy. However, it was the vote of clubs like ours that ultimately led to the change in policy, I am sure. I had become very popular in Rotary in Willingboro and, to a large extent, in Burlington County. When a conflict arose between Frank Quinn and another vocal member of the club, Willingboro municipal judge Uri Taenzer asked me to moderate a settlement of the issue at a special meeting held at Frank Quinn's home. It was settled peacefully and my skill at reconciliation was acknowledged gratefully.

When an African-American accused Frank Quinn's McDonald's restaurant in Burlington City of practicing racism, Frank did not know what to do. He alerted me and I agreed to look into the matter as a social scientist. I put together a team of researchers and conducted a participant observation study of the establishment over a time span sufficient to reach a conclusion. We determined that Frank Ouinn was operating a first-rate McDonald's, and any complaints of racism must have been an isolated incident. Racism was not characteristic of the establishment. Naturally, Quinn was pleased with the result of our investigation.

My involvement in the club, the township, and the county became more and more intense, but I was much younger and worked well under stress. However, I am not sure that I was prepared for the next surprise I encountered. It was 1971 and time for the election of new officers for the club. Frank Quinn, as president, was head of the nominating committee. When Frank Quinn called for the report, Marvin Ellis, the publisher of the *Burlington County Times*, was sitting beside me and whispered these words: "I am on the nominating committee and they never met. How can he give a report?"

Well, a report was given and those whom Frank wanted to serve in the positions he desired to serve were named. I was not re-nominated for the position of Community Service Director, nor was I nominated for a new position.

I immediately moved that the report of the nominating committee be received. I wanted to do three things with my motion. First, I wanted to show that I was in favor of supporting the candidates nominated by the committee; second, to show that I was moving to accept the report of the whole committee and was not angry because I was not re-nominated; and third, to allow discussion on Marvin's comment to me—that the committee had never met.

Someone seconded the motion and it was carried. But the problem was that Quinn never asked for questions or nominations from the floor. This was totally out of order. I spoke privately with Archie James, the third black person in Rotary, about the issue and he felt that what had happened was wrong. There were nearly a hundred people in that club and Marvin Ellis was not the only person on the nominating committee who refused to challenge Frank. None of the members of the committee would challenge him.

I decided that some action had to be taken in the name of justice. I sent a carefully drafted letter of resignation to each member of the club stating why I had resigned.

The new president wrote back that same day and asked that I offer an apology to Frank Quinn and the members of the club. I refused. Naturally, this meant that I would not be a Rotarian any longer. It really hurt because I had attended a Rotary Club meeting somewhere in the world without missing a single week for five years. I had perhaps brought back more flags from Rotary Clubs that I had attended than any other Rotarian. Giving this up was difficult, but the fight for justice was far more important.

Only two members ever spoke to me about my resignation. One was Dave Fisher, the owner of the Willingboro Chrysler Plymouth dealership, and the other was John Jordan, the owner of the Willingboro Hardware. I felt really bad about leaving the club because of the action of one man. And yet, that would have made all the difference in the world had it only been a matter of the action of one man. However, it was the inaction of nearly a hundred men, even the legitimate members of the nominating committee. All of them took part in the violation of Rotary's 4-test. The very first test was, "Is it true?" They failed that test because after receiving my letter everyone knew that I was correct in my argument, but no one was willing to stand up against Frank Quinn. Somehow, I had hoped that the executive committee would have at least challenged Frank and requested an apology or even called for a true meeting of the nominating committee. This did not happen, and I feel that some of the members must have been a bit burdened by this incident and were perhaps relieved that I did not remain in the club after the letter I sent.

What message was there in this for the club, then, and what message is there for the readers now? It seems that the message is the same. Either stand up for justice, a cause larger than yourself, or don't stand at all. By not standing, you essentially become a living apology for what you are and a poor excuse for what you ought to be. That happened to many Rotarians when they received my letter of resignation along with the allied explanations as to why I had felt it so important to resign. Would it have been different had I been white? We will never know, being that Frank Quinn had so much power at the time. But this incident is part of the history of Willingboro and it should be told. The sharing of the facts of what happened made me a rebel without a cause in the mind of Frank Quinn, at least. Yet it had to be done. African-Americans and whites, alike, need to know what unharnessed power can do in their town or anywhere in the state or nation.

However, the person who was affected even more than he would ever admit was Frank Quinn. I had accused him of using power that was not his to use for his personal satisfaction, a fact that was not denied or debated.

As this brief history is being written, it has been more than twenty years since I left the Willingboro Rotary Club. Those years have been filled with mixed emotions, bittersweet progress, strong opposition, and enthusiastic support for the role I played over the past two decades.

During this time, reapplying for membership in the Rotary Club was something that had crossed my mind from time to time. Ironically, I was proposed for membership in the Willingboro Rotary Club in 1999 by the pastor of the same church that proposed me for membership in 1969.

Each member had ten days to state in writing if they objected to my membership (standard procedure for Rotary Clubs). I was accepted as a new member in the spring of 1999. Since rejoining I have observed that the club is much smaller now and most of the members are new. Included now among the present membership are several women. The old members treat me with a sense of true welcome. I chose to come back for two reasons: one, I enjoyed Rotary and missed it very much; and two, I am rapidly winding down my ministry in the area and did not want this item to appear in the story of the African-Americans in Willingboro as a negative. By going back I hope that the readers will understand that it is never too late to make amends as long as the affected parties are there. By going back I have demonstrated that one cannot just preach forgiveness but must practice it also. None of the white people who were responsible for the 246 years of African slavery here in America are alive today.

Whites must be freed from the sins of their forefathers and of their own prejudices, and blacks must help liberate them through forgiveness, but this cannot happen until there is a willingness to work together toward a common solution to all problems. Both blacks and whites benefit when we can recognize our diversity, see the difference, and not let it make a difference.

Those who read about my going back to Rotary and see my willingness to put the past behind me should also put aside what may be keeping them from going that extra mile for justice, with the full understanding that it is either our fight or it is no one's fight.

The Continuing Crisis in Willingboro

B Y 1975-76, those persons who were committed to a kind of Theoretical Society of which the renown sociologist Robert Merton wrote about so extensively, one where there was a maintenance of the status quo or, in sociological terms, "pattern maintenance," were ready to acknowledge that Willingboro was facing a major problem, and the problem was within the schools.

This was consistent with what Levitt had projected when creating the community. He posited the idea that if there were problems in a new community, it would be with the schools. Thus, he envisioned a school in every park that operated around the clock 7 days a week, 365 days a year. This would be accomplished by making the school the center of all major activities for the community. They were designed and built to accommodate everything from regular instruction to community meetings and social gatherings.

Let's take a look at what Levitt said on the grand opening of Levittown in 1958:

> Problem number one in America today is schools. But in Levittown, New Jersey, there will be no such problems. We will build schools in every park that at completion will be turned over to the school board, lock, stock, and barrel, without one penny cost. The schools we will build represent the best thinking among educators, school planners, and architects today. The school built will provide complete flexibility in operation for any curriculum and any teaching technique. The classrooms are grouped around special use areas, which allow for separate, simultaneous teaching of very small groups or large ones of a hundred or more. A key of the building is interior courts, open to the sky which can be used in fair weather as outdoor classrooms or lecture areas.

Still another innovation is the extra auditorium called the

resources room. This is specially for use of new teaching techniques such as education films, recordings, and in-school TV.

It seems that Levitt thought of everything in planning the schools for Levittown, even though he was a little bit ahead of our high-tech-driven society. He wanted to solve each and every problem as the schools were built in order that no future problem would ever arise. Admittedly, Levitt did an excellent job in the planning of the schools in Willingboro, especially for his day. However, Levitt seemed to have forgotten one thing and did not perceive the other. What he forgot was that he was simply designing and constructing a building. It was the pupils, teachers, parents, administrators, and curriculum that would make the schools work for the community.

However, this was not really his problem. What Levitt did not perceive was equally important. The day would come when integration would be a part of life for the school system. And within twenty years, the majority of the schools would have a minority population and all of the variables associated with that transition. Not everyone acknowledged that Willingboro even had a problem. Township Manager John Tegley, who had been on the job for two years, referred to Willingboro in the mid-70s as the most active community around:

> A characteristic of this town has got to be the amount of community involvement. The level of participation is phenomenal .... Maybe it's because everyone enjoyed getting in on starting new groups because there were so many little children to keep busy, but the citizens who purchased Levitt homes wanted lots to do ... and they got it. There are 139 organizations listed in the 1974 edition of "Our Town," a yearly publication by the local Jaycees.... There really is something for everyone. If a private group doesn't provide it, the township will.... Without question, the largest such organization is the Police Athletic League, which involves thousands of boys and girls in its baseball, boxing, softball, soccer, track, basketball, and drum and bugle corps programs. P.A.L. even has its own office and staff to run its activities—and Willingboro is generous with its abundance. Most programs are open to out-of-township residents if there is space.... Willingboro is definitely where the action is."

I wonder if Tegley knew that he was speaking with blinders on; those who saw no problems at all were still in a dream, and those who saw a problem but felt that it was restricted to the schools were trying to suspend reality. In every instance, it was my judgment that they did not truly understand the problem confronting Willingboro. I believed that someone had missed the mark completely and others were way south of center and there was a need to challenge them to become more focused. First, it had to be pointed out that they were not coming to grips with the problem. Since the Letters to the Editor of the *Burlington County Times* is the most widely-read column of the paper, I decided to write a letter to the editor. This was in the winter of 1974. The letter is reproduced in its entirety below only because I was the first one to speak out in this vein and because the response was so swift and voluminous.

Unfortunately, as residents of Willingboro, we have been faced with the possibility of school busing, forced and voluntary, to correct the problem of racial imbalance in the Garfield East and Pennypacker schools.

I deemed this as unfortunate because busing is the wrong option for Willingboro. The lack of racial balance in our schools is symptomatic of a malignant problem in our community for which busing is not even an ameliorative treatment.

Willingboro is not a traditional suburban community, which arose as a result of a pattern of invasion, tipping point and succession, which took place. That is, Willingboro did not develop because blacks invaded the cities where whites lived in such numbers that the point of acceptability was tipped and the whites succeeded to Willingboro. Willingboro is itself a "transient center," without a stabilized housing market. This is due to the absence of sufficient locally based employment. Many of the traditional breadwinners are upwardly mobile and live here only until a transfer or a promotion comes through.

In such a community, members of all ethnic groups can live anywhere in apparent harmony because there are no entrenched ethnic or cultural interests nor direct implications for agitation or concerned action.

There is also a negative side to this quasi-utopia—an absence of a collective consciousness regarding the impact of one even upon the entire Willingboro community.

As a case in point—over a short span of years, Pennypacker has become a majority black park. Although we did not plan the happening, we did not plan for the prevention of it either. Next will be Garfield North, etc. Why is this going to happen?

Upward mobility–for both black and white workers. Whites will follow their jobs to other suburban communities and blacks will come to Willingboro from Philadelphia and Camden. Because blacks have fewer options than whites, they will stay in Willingboro longer, thus creating a rapid growth in the percentage of blacks in Willingboro.

Closing the Pennypacker school to avoid busing to achieve racial balance will solve the immediate school board problem, but would ultimately lead to an all-black park or an accelerated increase in the dependent welfare population there. Whites will not voluntarily let their children be bused and will therefore avoid Pennypacker, and middle-class blacks will command more expensive homes, thus causing more avoidance of Pennypacker (by whites and black middle class).

In summary, we have a problem in Willingboro and a solution must be found if we are to maintain an integrated community with great potential growth in an exemplary manner. To fail to find a solution is to plan, by default, for a Willingboro peopled by a majority black population without a bright future. However, to see this as a school problem, correctable by busing, forced or otherwise, is to misunderstand the process of economic development, community education and involvement as well as the function of the school.

During the weeks that followed my letter to the editor of the *BCT*, I received a large number of telephone calls, with most of the callers suggesting that I provide some additional rationale for my thinking.

In each instance, I promised that I would as time permitted. However it was two months before my schedule would allow for even a limited response. When I did get around to putting some thoughts on paper, the length was such that *BCT* was not an option for making them public. On the other hand, they were not sufficient for a major publication, so the decision was made to make a few dozen copies and pass them along to the stakeholders in the township.

In this response, I posited the hypothesis that the problem in Willingboro was not the racial imbalance in the schools; rather, it was one that resulted from economic choice and those elements related to economics, the least of which was the imbalance in the elementary school population. Thus, even if a total solution to the school problem were developed, it would only be a partial solution for Willingboro's problem as a whole.

In taking the position I did, I was aware of the dangers of stating too simply and too briefly complex problems that deserved careful research and scientific explanations.

However, I felt it necessary to offer at least another point of view concerning the problem of Willingboro since I cannot agree that it is in the area of racial imbalance in the schools and that it is correctable by the school board.

Again, I am going to set forth the entire text of that response.

In the paragraphs below, I have, with the letter to the editor, attempted to further redefine the problem facing Willingboro and offer some suggested solutions for deliberation and possible action by the total township.

I feel that the problem could and should be studied scientifically, for the benefit of our community and the greater benefit of humankind who may be similarly affected in other parts of this state and nation. However, in the absence of a systematic study based upon a scientific paradigm, I am offering the results of limited participant observation and casual analysis. This will be presented in an abbreviated chronological order to aid in the orderly presentation of the writer's points and hopefully help facilitate the reader's understanding of those points.

1. In 1955, the corporation Levitt and Sons, Inc., the nation's largest builder in the eastern United States, announced that it was going to build a new community in the Willingboro Township, northeast of the Standard Metropolitan Statistical Area (SMSA) of Philadelphia, Pennsylvania.

2. The proposed initial houses would range in price from $11,500 to $14,500. They would be built in parks of roughly 1,100 houses each and an elementary school, playground, and a swimming pool would be incorporated in each park. The houses were priced to attract buyers from the blue collar to the middle class.

3. The initial purchases of home sites in Willingboro were made in June 1958 by white families paying as little as $100 down. Homes were first occupied in October 1958, again by white families. At that time Levitt vowed that Willingboro would never be integrated. It must also be understood that the township officials had to agree with Levitt's discriminatory policies for him to be able to move forward with his building projects.

4. Levitt fought against the admission of blacks to Willing-boro all the way to the New Jersey State Supreme Court and only withdrew its case from the U.S. Supreme Court in 1960 when it was determined that integration was inevitable.

5. As late as 1964, there being only about 50 black families living in Willingboro, less than 1% of the total population. The educational and economic levels of blacks were substantially higher than whites at that time and remained so until the very early seventies.

6. Factors which contributed to the integration of Willingboro included:

   • Organized positive efforts on the part of religious groups such as Jews, Baptist ministers, and others, including the Human Relations Council and senators Case and Harrison Williams.

   • The New Jersey State law prohibiting racial discrimination in government-supported housing developments (FHA mortgage).

   • The higher quality of blacks who were screened as the initial purchasers.

   • The spatial layout of Willingboro into parks.

   • The absence of any entrenched ethnic or culturally threatening issues.

   • The mere fact that Willingboro was so new.

7. Other than Levitt and Sons, the corporate group of realtors was the only one who openly discriminated against blacks by refusing to show them houses. This may have been a combination of their own prejudices, and professional competition for the dollars from commissions. The latter was probably the stronger since there was the real danger of a white seller refusing to list a house which an agency had previously sold to blacks. In many instances, realtors promised to locate whites in parks where no blacks lived.

8. After 1965, blacks began to move into Willingboro in ever-increasing numbers, settling mostly in the older part of Pennypacker and to a lesser degree in other parts. There is some evidence that realtors influenced these patterns also.

9. By 1969, the blacks were moving into all parts of Willingboro. Although their numbers were growing, there were no attending problems of any significance associated with the influx of blacks.

10. By 1974, Willingboro reached its peak in population growth, household-wise; a suburban community due mainly to the fact that all construction has been completed and no new houses are planned.

11. The black sub-group has grown at a faster rate than the white population and/or the population of Willingboro in general, thus creating a disproportionate growth rate for blacks. (From less than 1% in the early sixties to more than 20% in the mid-seventies.)

12. In 1974, the median price of a new house was $41,000 in the U.S., a figure beyond the means of more than 90% of all black families.

13. Willingboro is perhaps still the only community that one can buy a relatively new home in a range from $30,000 to $40,000 and get the best buy for the amount invested. Thus Willingboro will still attract a large number of low and middle income blacks from the SMSA of Philadelphia. In the future this will reflect a change in the Puerto Rican influx into Willingboro as they make their flight from a deteriorated Camden, New Jersey.

14. In addition to the increasing number of black families moving into Willingboro, there are two other elements that must be factored into this picture. One, blacks tend to remain in Willingboro longer than whites because upward mobility for them is primarily reached with the escape from the ghettoes of Philadelphia, Trenton and Camden. Two, blacks tend to have larger dependent families than whites.

15. Whereas the total black population of Willingboro is in the 20% range, blacks make up 35% of the school population of the district due mainly to the fact referenced above.

16. For the blacks of Willingboro, this is decidedly a permanent bedroom community with few involved in full-time occupations here. (Most blacks moving into Willingboro already have stable employment.)

17. For the whites this is primarily a transient community,
    again with few, percentage-wise, involved in
    employment here. Whites are still upwardly mobile
    employment-wise.)

Most of the items mentioned above have combined in ways such
that definite problems are facing Willingboro as an integrated
suburban community. Attention will now be focused upon some of
those problems and a brief examination of the proposed solution
where one has been suggested. Additionally some suggestions will be
offered for a possible resolution of the perceived problem.

The number one problem facing Willingboro deals with the
problem of racial imbalance in the schools. This at least is the
position taken by the Willingboro School Board, the largest employer
in the township.

Willingboro is under a mandate to create a racial balance in its
school district. This basically means that the percentage of blacks in
any given school in the Willingboro district should not be the total
percentage of black pupils in the district as a whole. (With a variance
factor of 10%.)

Since the percentage of blacks in the district is presently 35%,
any school with a percentage of blacks greater than that has a problem
of racial imbalance. (Formula simply stated.)

The Pennypacker school for example has more than 50% blacks,
thus a racial imbalance situation faces our district and our community.
Other schools affected are Garfield, Garfield East, and Bookbinder.

The Suggested Solution (From the Board of Education)

1. The first step toward solving this problem from the
   school board's point of view would be to close the
   Pennypacker school.

2. Through a dual-provisions program, encourage parents
   in schools with less than 35% blacks, Garfield and
   Garfield East (control for the 10%), to voluntarily
   transfer their children to Pennypacker and Bookbinder
   vis-a-vis Pennypacker and Bookbinder to Garfield and
   Garfield East.

The second provision of the plan deals with what the board
refers to as the Attribution Plan. This means pre-assigning new
pupils coming into affected parks to schools that will help to
alleviate the racial imbalance in the affected schools.

Implementation: Notify all realtors that this will be done so the new arrivals to Willingboro will be prepared to have their children bused before they move to an affected part.

Assumptions built into the board's plan and author's reaction in parentheses.

A. That parents will voluntarily allow their children to be bused. (All available data indicate that the contrary is true especially among whites. Thus, provision two is perceived as not workable.)

B. That white realtors can be expected to help implement the plan without bias. (Remember, it was the realtors who openly practiced discrimination when Willingboro was going through its integration pains.) The reason then was mainly economic and what evidence is there that the situation has changed?

C. That white parents will allow their children to be bused to other parts in order to live in Willingboro. (This does not control for two factors: whites have always been opposed to busing and two, they have more options to move into other communities.) My fear is that short of a scientific study to prove otherwise, this will only increase the number of black residents in Willingboro.

This proposal fails to recognize that the possible domino effect (borrowing a militaristic concept) may hasten the day when all the parks will be over the 35% blacks allowed by state law. Then what, busing for the entire community? (Busing will then involve communities outside of Willingboro.)

If this seems absurd or unduly pessimistic, just take a look at what is happening in the Garfield North school. In 1969, the total student population was 1% black, in 1971, 10% black and in 1976, 24% black. (From my driveway on a corner in Garfield North, I have observed more than a dozen white families moving out and in every instance except two, they were replaced by blacks.)

None of the blacks have moved since the first family came within my view on August 9,1969. We moved to Garfield North on August 8, 1969. When I looked through a realtor's Multiple Listing Service (MLS) book recently, I could see why this was happening. As indicated, the best buy for the money was still in Willingboro through the decades of the sixties and seventies.

Let it be quickly added that I feel that the school board has done a creditable job in assuming and handling a problem that belongs to all of us. However, their solution is more of a holding pattern than a real solution.

I feel that Willingboro, as a united community, should take an unequivocal position that whereas Willingboro is not a true "heaven," it is not a segregated community and any racial imbalance in our school system is the result of social economic factors which are not controllable by us. We, therefore, will not ever be able to achieve a racial balance in the schools in my opinion nor should the same be a top priority.

This stance should get broad community-based support through an opinion or attitudinal survey scientifically conducted. If the people of Willingboro, black and white, would rather see us do some things constructively for our community other than dissipate our energy and spend our dollars on attempts to satisfy a law that should not be applied to Willingboro in the first place, then let us take our case all the way to the U.S. Supreme Court and seek to overturn all lower court decisions once and for all.

An alternative suggestion, only if we lack the courage for the first, is to establish a highly efficient system of pre-education of all realtors regarding the attribution plan and develop effective ways of monitoring the same to make sure that a scientific evaluation can be made after the first and second year of implementation. If the results are negative at that time, then we should resort to the above suggestion.

Other problems facing Willingboro:

A. Presently existing problems.

  1. Black families compose more than 20% of the population of Willingboro and the rate is increasing annually.

  2. There are only two or three black owned and operated businesses in the township. This estimate was due to the fact of being uncertain regarding one business.

  3. The practicing residential professional blacks in Willingboro are limited to teachers and a few nurses. Exact data was impossible to obtain at this time.

  4. Blacks frequent the businesses that sell goods and professionals that render services and are, in 99% of the cases, greeted by white salespersons and receptionists.

  5. Willingboro has a township council composed of five white persons and to this day has never had a black member.

6. Were it not for a decision of the board, where one black person was named to a vacancy, an all-white board would be making school policy affecting a school system that is 35% black.

7. A volunteer fire department is staffed by whites only based upon available data.

8. Over twenty business establishments in the immediate Willingboro area that employ more than twenty persons each have been identified but not one employee is a black person.

9. Therefore, when a black calls a doctor, a lawyer, the police, a department store, an auto dealership, the hospital, a restaurant, the fire department, a dentist, service station, a bank, etc., in Willingboro, the chances are not only that the voice that answers will be white but the people who render service will also be white.

B. Prognosis for the future is not positive under existing circumstances.
If the U.S. Supreme Court forces Willingboro to allow realtors to again place their "For Sale" signs on lawns, there will be a certain increase in percentage of black population growth.

C. An increase in the welfare-dependent population, due to the absence of good jobs for blacks and other poor here in Willingboro is a certainty.

D. A continuing lack of sensitivity to the need for some well-planned community-based activities geared to meet all age groups will further prevent the creation of a well-balanced integrated community. Willingboro is integrated but not inclusive. Thus, when all factors are considered, the future is not bright for Willingboro as an inclusive community.

Some Suggestions for Meaningful Change in Willingboro:

A. Make a deliberate effort to get blacks registered to vote and participate in the total life structure of Willingboro. This should be a community-wide effort with the *Burlington County Times* providing ample coverage to the matter. Efforts in this regard could be enhanced through the existing organizations such as PAC, religious places of worship, Rotary Club, etc.

B. Work with concerned organizations to seek the
employment of qualified blacks, in representative
numbers, in all business establishments that now exclude
them and seek the upgrading of others.

C. Begin an active campaign, through the township council,
board of education, religious groups, and the private sector
to help promote better human relations among all people
of Willingboro. This is not to suggest that we have a
profile of protest here, rather to indicate that there is little
"community" feeling among the citizens of Willingboro.

D. Actively recruit black professionals to come to Willingboro
to practice their disciplines. This can be aided through the
assistance of predominantly black colleges, hospitals
where black doctors are doing their internships, the
NAACP, Urban League, etc.

F. Seek more black administrators for the school system. This
can be done through the upgrading of qualified blacks
presently on staff as well as recruiting others.

G. Upgrade some black police to officer ranks. If the passing
of the Civil Service Test is a problem, then provide test
help centers the same as is done for doctors, lawyers, etc.,
that are utilized by whites.

H. Encourage the volunteer fire department to have
orientation programs where blacks can become familiar
with the various aspects of that service and develop an
interest to participate.

The *Burlington County Times* should become more determined
in its efforts to recruit blacks. Black newspapers and journalism
schools will cooperate with them when they know what we are
trying to do. Looking at the pictures portrayed in the *BCT* and
many of the non-crime related articles, one could easily conclude that the publisher and/or reporters are racist or there are
no blacks doing anything worthy of print. In reality, neither idea
is absolutely true. Perhaps it should be remembered that blacks
read the white papers as well as black publications.

I. Banks should place qualified blacks on their board of
directors even if the normal financial requirement for such a
seat must be lowered or waived.

All of the established, generally recognized denominational churches have white ministers except one. This is the way it has always been since the establishment of Willingboro. (The lone black pastor was not by design of Levitt rather by decisions made by a group of blacks to start their church.)

Black ministers should be called as associates. This is especially true for Baptist, Methodist and Catholic groups since more blacks attend those services as supporting members.

Again, blacks are very sensitive regarding their religion and need to relate to a black minister at least occasionally. It is in these areas that I see the real problem facing Willingboro. If we do not control for this problem now, the negative effects of a black population in Willingboro of over 50% must be shared by those who move away as well as those who have stayed behind.

When this happens, and it is projected to happen by 1982 if preventive measures are not taken, we can expect three significant happenings: one, more rapid exodus of whites moving out of Willingboro, as of whites moving into Willingboro; two, a closing of some service orientated businesses on the plaza; and three, a negative shift in nature of tax rates. More specifically, the rate for homeowners will soar as businesses close and leave the township and are not replaced. Obviously, there is a multitude of allied problems associated with this last reference.

Let me conclude these scattered thoughts with three observations. One, a study should be conducted to test the points presented here. Two, I recently sat in a business establishment until twenty (20) customers had come through the door; nine (9) were black and eleven (11) were white. Not one of the people employed was black. Thinking that may have been an unusual day, I went back two weeks later and the ration had changed a little; it was now ten blacks out of the first twenty customers that entered the establishment.

Three, now is the time for all the citizens of Willingboro to get together to look at ourselves before this profile becomes a reality with which we cannot survive and Willingboro will never be transformed from a community of strangers into an inclusive community. The task belongs to all of us and I know that we have the way to do it and hope that we have the will. But we had better hurry.

Burlington County Times Publisher
Lauds Willingboro

M ANY LEADERS in the community felt that a problem existed in Willingboro and that it was related primarily to the schools. Their case had been made as early as 1976. I assumed the position that the problem was far more widespread than the realm of the schools, and that it began before 1976. It basically included the total fabric of Willingboro and was in some degree incorporated in the town's inception. Here we have one instance that was supported by the majority of those who were speaking out holding to the view that the problem, though unsolved, was localized. At the other polar extreme was my own lone voice claiming that the problem was widespread and that there were no noticeable signs of anything being done to find solutions. Who was correct? Perhaps that would have made an interesting debate. Instead of a debate, enter Marvin Ellis, the publisher of the *Burlington County Times*, saying in a special message to the people of Willingboro in 1978 that there was not really any problem at all.

Because his message was supported by the media that was under his control and by a myriad of personal contacts within the township, who would want to question his message to a community when they needed it the most?

His message is represented below, just as it appeared on October 17, 1978.

Enthusiasm, pride, commitment ... these are the qualities that make Willingboro great.

The citizens of Willingboro are enthusiastic about their beautiful town, their fantastic recreation program, their fine schools and involved churches.

They are proud of the example they have set in bringing together people of all races, religions, income levels, and national backgrounds. They have proved that such a community can not only live together in harmony, but can also work together on such outstanding community events as the International Festival, the Fourth of July parade, and the Fun Day in the Park.

Most importantly, Willingboro citizens are committed to facing their problems and solving them. [Perhaps this is why he says there are not any.] While some communities have a tendency to brush their problems under a rug, Willingboro is highly articulate in outlining their problems and working towards a sensible solution. Willingboro's municipal government, as a result, has served as a model of how a local government should be operated.

The past 20 years have been Willingboro's formative years. The problems of building and operating a modern community of almost 50,000 people have been faced, and for the most part, solved.

The people of Willingboro have built strong foundations that should guarantee even better years ahead.

That really leaves nothing to be said. Ellis has said it all. But has he really? While this message was being released, lauding the racial harmony in the township, the fine schools, and involved churches, one African-American church, Saints Memorial, was struggling to find a place to build a permanent facility in a town that made no provisions for such churches. A second African-American church, Alpha, was doing battle with the Zoning Board of Adjustment seeking a variance to allow for an addition on its small facility, and a third African-American church, Cathedral of Love, was having difficulties just trying to get started.

Also in tandem with the message from the publisher, whites had begun to move out of the town as more blacks moved in. Equally important was the upcoming crisis that had already begun to surface concerning the survival of the Willingboro Plaza.

I spoke to Marvin as a friend after his message to the people and reminded him of these very facts. His response as I recall was, "Well, Joe, you don't want people to get anxious about the negative, do you?" Anxious about the negative? Then I remembered, but did not say anything about it. He had been the one who told me that Frank Quinn had bypassed the nominating committee of the Rotary Club and made a personal report to the club, which resulted in my taking leave from the club. Was he operating on the principle of don't get people anxious about the negative? Where in this world has there ever been meaningful and substantial change without some conflict? Perhaps I was wrong, but I did not pursue the issue any further with Ellis. I really did not need to. I believed that I was correct and the problems in Willingboro were not nonexistent because they had been dealt with. They were minimal in the eyes of those who saw a problem at all because they, like Ellis, did not want to get the people anxious about the negative.

Three Willingboro Politicians Lose Bid
for Higher Office

FRANK QUINN, the champion of charitable causes, the owner of multiple McDonald's, a Willingboro councilman, president of the Willingboro Rotary Club, campaign chairman of United Way of Burlington County, perhaps the most visible person in the local Democratic Party, decided in the 1980's that his gifts and skills were needed in Trenton. In deciding to run for a seat in the New Jersey Senate, Quinn, by his own private admission, was making an initial installment on a political future that went much further than the New Jersey Senate.

It would seem that this would have been an easy win for Quinn. He had name recognition, solid backing from Willingboro and the Democratic Club, good support from the rest of the district, and plenty of funding. He ran a highly visible campaign, being perhaps the first to use a large panel truck with "QUINN FOR SENATE" painted on either side. This truck went throughout the election district. Additionally, there were rallies, campaign speeches, and media blitzes. However, in the end, Quinn lost. The defeat was perhaps not only more than he expected, but more than he could handle. He was not accustomed to losing anything. Maybe he thought that the defeat would not set well with his colleagues. The despondent Quinn soon sold his two McDonald's restaurants in the area and moved to another town out of the district. He is occasionally seen around the area, but no one mentions his name.

Quinn had fallen hard, but there was not as large a vacuum in the local political arena as one might have expected. His strongest ally, Bill Kearns, who was slightly in Quinn's shadow as Quinn made a name for himself, rose immediately to the top of the political sphere and remains there today, although he does not hold a political *office*.

Kearns did run for political office himself almost twenty years ago. He ran for the congressional seat from the sixth district, a position held by Edwin B. Forsythe of Moorestown. Kearns had the strongest backing possible from the municipality of Willingboro, and the heavy weights like Catherine A. Costa and Dr. Charles Ehrlich changed their minds about running against him in the June primary. Kearns was young, thirty-four years old at the time, energetic, and ambitious. He was willing to work hard, but did not realize how hard one would have to work to unseat a Republican in Burlington County's sixth district. In the end, Forsythe handed

Kearns a resounding defeat. But unlike his close friend and ally Frank Quinn, Kearns did not let this defeat cause him to pick up his marbles and run out of town. Instead, he simply dug in deeper into the fertile ground of Willingboro, where he was content to make his operational base for the indefinite future. Here he knew who was "king of the hill," and anyone who wanted to hold any office in town, political or professional, if it related or relates to the township proper, then Kearns is somewhere in the shadows influencing every decision and every election.

In saying this, I must quickly add that Kearns is not a vindictive person and has been helpful to more than a few people in town. Bill Kearns has also used his influence to save the township a lot of embarrassment and money, especially as it has concerned the Alpha Church and the Zoning Board of Adjustment. This will be referenced in another section of this writing.

Over the past twenty years, a number of die-hard Republicans or switch-over Republicans have run for township council. Only one candidate is being mentioned in this setting because he seemed to have been the most sincere and the best prepared to run for a seat on the council in a town that is well-known for its blind Democratic loyalty. That person is African-American Levi Bizzelle, a switch-over Republican. He charges, and there is some evidence to support the same, that he was not treated fairly by the Democrats. However, what he did not know was that one can be wrong and a Democrat in Willingboro and still win.

Bizzelle brought one of the strongest backgrounds to the candidacy of a seat on council than anyone elected in the last twenty years. He is a veteran of twenty-four years of distinguished service during which he served as a member of the Special Forces in Vietnam. He is a former member of the New Jersey Advisory Board for Probation, having been appointed by the Chief Justice. Bizzelle was Chief of Police at the Philadelphia Naval Shipyard, training director at the Federal Law Enforcement Training Center while serving as a special police officer for Willingboro, and a senior corrections officer at Trenton State Prison. Furthermore, he launched and directed a number of youth programs. Bizzelle also has a master's degree in criminal justice and taught criminal justice as an adjunct professor at Jersey City State College. This is just a little of Bizzelle's background. He was willing to serve on council and donate his pay to charity. He had some definite proposals for the revitalization of Willingboro Plaza on Route 130. But he had a dilemma: he was a Republican. The fact that there was a Democrat running for re-election from the same church did not help or hurt his efforts. He simply did not have enough money, time, or the proper backing of the Republicans for him to win. It is possible for a Republican to win a seat on council and it will probably happen, but it will not be until the African-Americans in Willingboro begin to listen to the message and not the rhetoric, and vote for the candidate and not the party.

Another African-American who ran a serious campaign for office in the county, but was unsuccessful, is the Reverend Ernest Light, pastor of the Good Shepherd Church.

It is worth noting that there have been African-Americans on the Willingboro Township Council for the past twenty years. However, in each instance, they were first appointed to fulfill someone's unexpired term and later ran as an incumbent.

The time has not yet come for some new innovation into the political structure, where candidates can launch out into the deep political waters of Willingboro, paddling their own oars without sitting in the back of the canoe being guided by old-guard Democrats. It is this kind of change that is needed in Willingboro.

Township Council Gives Itself a Failing Mark

IN REFUSING to appoint Eddie Durham as mayor of Willingboro in 1983 in the rotation pattern it had long followed, the township council deserves a failing grade as a fair and impartial governmental body. Instead, it proved itself to be an interlocking directorate and a power elite in the style of Friedrich Nietzsche, where only the best and the purest deserve to survive.

It is true that Durham had been jointly under investigation with his wife in the case of the abuse of a child entrusted to their care. His wife subsequently pleaded guilty to "over-punishing" the little girl on several occasions, which resulted in the girl being hospitalized in a semi-comatose state with severe fractures, brain and kidney damage, and multiple bruises.

Who would doubt that this were not a very serious matter when the life of a child was at stake and even threatened? However gaudy the details of that case, the seriousness of the harm to the child, and the chilling charges against the Durhams were, they should not loom greater than the fact of law in our judicial system.

Durham had been acquitted months before the stated election on all charges of abuse, neglect, and endangering the life of the child who was staying in their home. Not only that, but the year before he had allowed his name to be withdrawn from the annual rotation among council members for the one-year mayoral term while the investigation was still underway. This was a fine gesture and must have been deemed the appropriate thing to do by Durham. One can be sure that he and his wife went through punishment to fit the crime before the verdicts were rendered, and they would have to live with whatever the verdict was for a while into the future.

However, an acquittal means that the slate is wiped clean, that there was not enough evidence to convict, and that the accused could be restored to the position that was his before the charges were filed and the trial held. Council did not deem it appropriate for Durham to step down when he and his wife were under investigation. In fact, they supported him in the belief that he was innocent. What is even more peculiar in this scenario is that the only requirement for the position of mayor is that one be a member of council and receive three or more votes. This had never been an issue until this particular event.

The reason that this is put in the category of a Nietzsche-type pattern is because suddenly the members of council had become so pure, so innocent, so above reproach. The only difference was that Nietzsche would have stated up front that Durham had ceased to meet his standards. He was just that arrogant and honest, whereas the members of council were not. They did two things that were inappropriate and bordered on dishonesty. One, they claimed to have received so many calls from the public they represented, and the hue and cry was for them not to vote for Durham as mayor, when, in fact, very few people knew enough about the system to even know or care who was going to be mayor. The people of Willingboro, did not see the position of mayor as having any power within the political system. Willingboro is laid out in 11 self-contained parks and the members of council are elected at large but do not serve at the pleasure of a given park or even the electorate when it comes right down to the real crux of the political structure.

The members of council serve themselves and they have virtually always been in agreement even in this instance with Durham. It seems very strange that one day before the stated election, the *BCT* reported that two council members had indicated that the vote would be five to zero to elect Durham. What happened to change the vote to four-zero with one abstaining? Did the members get all of those calls in one day? That is doubtful.

The second thing that this group did that was a departure from the strong and forthright position of a Friedrich Nietzsche was that they waited until the vote was cast before Durham knew that he was going to be taken out of rotation for the mayoral position for another year. How did they think Durham could have lived with that? After all, he had his biological family, his pastor, and members of his faith community present to witness the moment. A celebration had been planned for Durham after the swearing-in ceremony at the Saints Memorial Community Church, where Durham served as associate pastor. To deny Durham the right to be mayor when the people were not demanding that he resign from the position of councilman was wrong. One wonders who all these people were who allegedly contacted the members of council in regards to this issue. As I recall, I was president of the Willingboro Clergy Association and we did not take a negative position on this issue, and we represented more people than any other group in town.

The fact that the council turned down some requests and voted against some concerns when there was an unquestionable public position opposite to the one that they took shows that they were more of an elitist club than honest politicians.

Could the Reverend Ken Pipes have been more on target than the council was willing to admit when he sent a letter to the council that was endorsed by the Willingboro Clergy Association in March of 1980? Here are a few quotes from that letter:

> As I understand the root meaning of the word 'politics,' it means simply that which concerns the lives of people in a given area .... It is comprised of concerns which affect all the people, not just a few.... As far as possible, the decisions which of necessity must be made by the elected representatives ought to be made with the interest of the whole people in mind. When controversial, as well as non-controversial issues arise, it would seem expedient that widely diverse segments of the population would be sought out for consultation and input prior to the formulation of policies and the adoption of positions which impact upon the lives of people... Are you, as leaders, elected to represent the people of our community, or to seek your own interest?

This letter drew negative reactions from a council where Eddie Durham was still a member. Little did Durham know that a year later he would be out of the club of the elite and the council would be back to business as usual and his non-selection as mayor would be trashed the same way Pipes' letter was trashed.

Perhaps both Durham and Pipes were correct, but they went up against a Goliath and did not have a rock in their sling.

Working and Serving in the Community

Black Leaders in Burlington County

As THIS TREATISE is being penned, more discoveries are being made of African-Americans who have, in ways large and small, made a contribution to the total development of Willingboro. Should this effort be postponed until the research is exhausted, it probably would never be written. There does not exist a book on the subject, and there are no persons who have been around long enough to provide an unbroken reference to black leaders. Some of the persons, who have been and will be mentioned, lived outside of Willingboro or lived in the township but made their contribution throughout the county. Although the greater emphasis of this writer is directed toward Willingboro, there will of necessity be a cross-fertilization of township lines as this record unfolds.

Recently, Wayne Browne, the African-American staff writer for the *Burlington County Times*, lifted up some names of key black leaders of the past and present, along with those whom he considers to be future leaders. Those names were familiar to me because they can be found in the Marabash Museum in New Egypt. Heading his list were the Reverend Walter A. Rice, David Parker, and Dr. James Still. However, the problem with mentioning the names of past leaders of any ethnic group is closely related to the fact that not much is written about them. History oftentimes is more subjective than objective. It comes down to the point where it is "his-(s)tory." This has been true of the textbooks used in our public schools for over one hundred years. Only within the last thirty years have we begun to rewrite history to provide for African-Americans the proper place that they should have in the history of this nation. One minor case in point is the National Colored/Negro Baseball League. Were it not for the fact that my brother-in-law played on the National Colored/Negro Baseball League more than fifty years ago, I would not have known about the league at all because the information was not included in the history textbooks written by white historians that were used in the segregated schools I attended.

Another example right here in Burlington County is the Reverend Walter A. Rice (1845-1899), who founded the Manual Training and Industrial School in Bordentown in 1866, just a few years after the end of slavery. Rice had the vision of his race extending their contributions beyond the levels provided by the regular schools for colored. The school he founded was to extend that vision by providing opportunities for young blacks to advance educationally beyond the fifth grade while at the same time learning a useful trade. The school won the acclaim of the New Jersey State Legislature and rose to the statute of being referred to as the Tuskegee of the North, due mainly to the excellent program and developmental coaching provided by Dr. Booker T. Washington, founder of Tuskegee of Alabama. This one leader has been singled out from the past because the buildings that housed the Manual Training and Industrial School in Bordentown still stand. Although they are mostly empty, structurally they appear to be quite capable of being completely restored and used. What better place to house the Marabash Museum than in one of those buildings, as the museum founders have been trying for years to achieve?

Burlington County Community Action Program

I T WAS SUGGESTED in 1974 that I become a member of the Board of Trustees of the Burlington County Community Action Program (BCCAP) because they could use a person with my skills. Around that time I had a trip planned for California, and while there I met with some of the people in the Watts section of Los Angeles, the area that was the hardest hit by the recent riots.

Looking at the devastation that was left behind in the riot-torn area, I saw the need for a united effort, involving all segments of the community, if the community were going to be restored. Many people were already working together to help rebuild what was damaged or destroyed by the riots. I impressed upon those present that the challenges that lay ahead of them would take more than what they had already given in time and energy. It would take a revolution of the heart of all people in southern California, in cooperation with the state and federal government, to accomplish the kind of rebuilding that was needed. Well, that was their problem and I left it with them and headed back to New Jersey.

I decided to accept the invitation to serve on the BCCAP Board of Trustees. Little did I realize it, but I was walking into a virtual lion's den without any prior preparation. A number of factors were operating at the same time, each one with the potential of destroying the only program for the poor in Burlington County. There was the issue with the executive director, who was being accused of everything from poor management to the misuse of staff by having them do work at his private home. The bookkeeping department was in a shambles, and it was quite evident that the board was divided into two factions, and within these two factions there were other divisions.

I deemed it appropriate to try to learn more of the facts before getting too involved in the fray. So I arranged my schedule to be in New Jersey as much as I could over the next two months in order to become more informed about what was really going on with the BCCAP agency and with the Board of Trustees. It was then that I learned that there were two other key players, the Office of Economic Opportunity (OEO) and the Board of Chosen Freeholders of Burlington County. Each player wanted to see the agency operating according to their own concepts of how things should be done.

Unfortunately, all of these players had power, and there seemed to be little room for a neutral voice, even if there were one. Each meeting, which was held monthly, was characterized by posturing, fighting, and threats of takeover by the Freeholders, if the federal government did not do it first.

It seemed to me that the best place for my input and perhaps the best place to start unraveling the many tangled threads of confusion was with the director, who was, after all, the one charged with the responsibility of directing the agency, regardless of the cloud of suspicion surrounding his position. After speaking with him for several hours on several occasions, I learned that there were some grounds for some of the charges and that a grand jury would most certainly come up with evidence sufficient for him to go on trial. If enough evidence was found for his case to go to trial, and he were found guilty, it would be the death-nail for the agency for sure, and a bad mark on the larger black community, since the director was also a pastor.

Sure enough, the prosecuting attorney did call for a grand jury to hear the evidence in the case. I went to the director and requested that he resign immediately. By resigning, he would, perhaps, lighten the blow of any findings of the grand jury. His words were, "What if I resign and they screw me anyway?" He was referring as much to his opponents who had been called to testify as he was to the Freeholders, who seemingly wanted him out as well.

He agreed to resign, and I called a meeting to inform the board so we could seek an interim executive director. I also wanted to get a feel for what had been told to the grand jury. I knew that none of them had been sequestered, and they would be arguing about what should be done with the executive director even with his resignation on the table. By this time, I was president of the board, so I let them talk past midnight. When the meeting was over, I not only knew what those who had not yet testified were going to say, but also what had already been said to the grand jury. This was very helpful to my plan of action before the grand jury since I was the last person to testify. In my heart and mind, I knew that there was no way that the evidence given to the grand jury through the sworn statements of those who had a grudge against the executive director or against the agency was going to have ultimate sway over the decision of the grand jury. Through the grace of God, my testimony was such that doubts were placed upon all of the others who had given negative testimony, and the result was that the grand jury was discharged without rendering an indictment against the executive.

Although I am not providing the content of my testimony given before the grand jury, this much can be stated. Although the executive director was guilty of ineptitude and a couple of errors, in his heart he was a good man and had given leadership to the agency all of the years and should have his resignation accepted for personal reasons, and let the case be at rest.

Actually this was what happened, as there were too many other issues confronting the agency to be spending time on a matter that was now history. (The executive Director went on to become first a Presiding Elder and then a bishop in the African Methodist Episcopal Zion Church, a position which he still holds).

The next project facing my presidency was to try to bring some harmony to the board. This was extremely important because the friction on the board was long-standing and opinions were deeply rooted among the two sides. Even while this effort was going forward, we needed an executive director for the agency. Out of a small pool of candidates, another preacher was called to head the agency. Although I thought the choice of candidate was a poor one, it was not the time to exercise any influence as the president of the board, so I voted to accept the recommendation of the personnel committee. I didn't expect it to be long before the new executive director made some serious management errors.

The new executive director began firing persons he did not personally like and hiring those whom he did. In the meantime, nothing was being done with the bookkeeping department because the new executive director dismissed the bookkeeping department. This and other instances of poor judgment caused the board to put the executive director on a sixty-day probation period, with the understanding that he could be discharged within that time if definite improvements were not made.

The *Burlington County Times* covered each issue, and the press we received was negative. OEO offered to send the agency someone who could serve as a consultant while we worked out our problems. We welcomed the help, and a very good consultant was appointed to assist us with problems in the office and with the staff. This allowed me to focus on trying to unify the two factions of the board, which had deteriorated to such an extent that we were having separate meetings. I later learned that the Freeholders were behind a lot of the division because they wanted to get rid of me. In fact, the Freeholders removed me from the board as their appointee and replaced me with another person.

At the same meeting when this happened, a member of the board, who was also a minister, had resigned because he was being transferred to a church out of the state. I was chosen to take his position. The Freeholders tried to block this, but my knowledge of parliamentary procedure was keen enough to know that we were operating within our rights as a board. I called for a legal opinion from the attorney, who was present at the meeting, and my position was supported. This was all that I needed to begin to exert the kind of leadership that was needed to bring the two factions together.

The first thing we had to do, which was loudly objected to by the Freeholders, was to close the door to the press. To justify my action, I pointed out that the press had reported, "OEO to appoint BCCAP director." I knew that this was not true because what they had offered us was a consultant, which we needed. Not only that, neither the OEO nor the Freeholders had the authority to appoint a director. This was a board decision as stated in our bylaws. Besides, we were a New Jersey corporation and the only thing that the local or state governments could do would be to withhold funding. Naturally this would hurt the agency and cause us to shut down voluntarily or at least greatly cut back on our programs, as most of our $2 million annual budget came by way of public funding. However, I never did really believe they would do that. It would start a race war larger than anything that the county had seen, and those politicians did not want that. They especially did not want to do battle with me on an issue of that magnitude. In spite of this apparent balance of power between the president of the BCCAP board and the board of Freeholders, I also knew that the agency depended upon us getting our house in order.

As expected, the decision to keep the press out upset the leader of the personnel committee. So she held a few private meetings in her home discussing ways that she could bring trouble to the agency and cause my name to be tarnished. Not only did the word get back to me, but the clandestine meetings were secretly recorded on tape and given to me. I played part of the tape at the next meeting and that was the end of that lady and the true beginning of a renewal of the board.

During the next several months we met as a joint board, and then as a united board, often as frequently as weekly. The consultants were a great help, and when they left, they publicly stated that the agency would be well-served if I would resign from the board and take over the role of executive director. There were rows of cheers from the board members. It was kind of the board members to think that highly of me, but I declined the invitation.

By the time we opened the meetings to the public again in mid-1974, all of the animosity had left the board and the agency's house was in order. Feeling that my mission was over, I went on to other areas of service to the people of Burlington County and Willingboro, feeling confident that the BCCAP had a board and staff ready to do the same.

The board called the Reverend Silas Townsend as the next executive director, and he has served well up to this day. Not many people today are aware of just how close BCCAP was to being taken over by the white ruling class. They may even have reopened it with an African-American executive director, but it would have been one who was under their direct control. The thought of saving the only major program in the county operated for the poor and predominantly run by African-Americans was more important to me than the challenge to my own reputation, which occurred several times during the struggle to save it.

As to the former executive director, he went on to become a presiding elder in his denomination and is now a bishop. Who knows, perhaps he never would have become a bishop had he remained with BCCAP. Maybe it is true, that all things are well that end well.

While engaging in the battle with the board of Freeholders while President of BCCAP, my name was kept before the people via the press. This can account for so many calls for help I received from so many different segments of the country.

Fighting Discrimination
at McGuire Air Force Base

B EING ACTIVE in the community, I'd heard of a number of complaints of African-Americans being discriminated against at the McGuire Air Force Base. However, there was never enough evidence for the PNBC Home Mission Board office, that I, at this time headed, to get involved, especially since we did not have a base chaplain with whom I could relate. Things changed when in 1975 John Collier came to my office without an appointment and asked to see me.

He was a tall, slender man, not well dressed, but clean. He humbly thanked me for taking the time to see him and promised to be very brief. In a short time, Collier shared his problem and his heart. He had been employed by the McGuire Air Force Base as a civilian aircraft mechanic, a position that he had held for several years. According to Collier, he had been an exemplary employee and had always received high praise on his performance evaluations. However, in the last six months a new supervising sergeant had taken over his unit. Although Collier's work ethic had remained the same, the new sergeant had given him a very unfavorable rating, which Collier refused to sign. He was put on probation for refusing to sign.

He indicated that a few other African-Americans had also been written up unfairly, but they had signed their documents out of fear that they would lose their jobs if they did not. Most of them thought the sergeant was racially biased against blacks but could not prove it.

Rather abruptly, Collier got to his point. He had been dismissed from his job due to some trumped-up charges that were blown out of proportion. His story went something like this: Collier worked the evening shift, 4 p.m. to midnight. However, on the day of the incident, he worked a double, which kept him on the job until 8 a.m. the following day. He admitted that he was tired when the second shift ended and just wanted to go home to get some sleep. He was almost off the base when he was ordered to pull over by two military policemen, both white. They ordered Collier out of the car and searched his car and body. They did not tell Collier why they pulled him over or why they were searching him. When the searches were over, they found a half pack of cigarettes, a few dollars and change, and allegedly four marijuana cigarettes in a small pouch in the glove compartment. They handcuffed Collier and drove him back to the base police station. There he was charged with possession of an illegal substance. He was told to report to his supervisor before coming back to work. Collier was released, and he had to walk back to his car where he had been pulled over.

Worried and weary, Collier drove home and told his wife, Miss Freddie, what had happened. He told her not to worry, and reassured her that he would certainly be cleared when he reported to work that afternoon. He was not cleared but suspended. He was told that an administrative hearing would be held and the outcome would determine his future. Within two weeks, the administrative hearing was set, and the result was strong and negative. Collier was dismissed from his job and told that he could not work in any unit dealing with aircraft again. Collier tried to explain that he had not been smoking the marijuana, and that there were two joints in the pouch, not four as claimed.

Over the next several months Collier turned to every agency he knew, or heard of, trying to get help. His union had been on the case for months, with no results. He was advised that it was best to drop the matter and try to find employment elsewhere, either on the base or out in the public sector. He had tried both unsuccessfully. He contacted the NAACP and they were not interested in his case, and the ACLU did not deem it worthy of their involvement. He wrote the legislatures in the New Jersey State Senate asking for help, to no avail. The same was true when he wrote the two U.S. senators from New Jersey and his congressman. There was no response from any of them. Collier showed me copies of letters he had written to the persons mentioned.

Then Collier showed me a letter from Senator Edward Kennedy in Washington. The letter thanked Collier for contacting him and promised to look into the matter as soon as possible. Although nothing else was done about it from Kennedy's office, Collier was proud that he had received a response from someone who was not even from the State of New Jersey. I certainly did not want to deflate what little ego Collier had left by suggesting that Senator Kennedy probably never heard of him. The letter was most likely a form letter sent by an aide in order to tabulate the number of contacts the senator made with the public. Even so, it was the only response he had received and the letterhead was impressive.

To this day, I am not completely sure why I agreed to look into the matter for Collier. I did not know him, had never heard of him, and he did not live in Willingboro. He lived in Mt. Holly where he and his family had been associated with a church of another denomination, although he was not at all active. And I've always had a zero tolerance for illegal drug use. Yet, I recognized that this incident was not about the drug use, but about discrimination. There was something about the man that led me to believe him, and I thought I should try to do something.

I asked Collier to drive me out to the base so I could talk with his former supervising sergeant. He said that he would, but it was not worth the time since the sergeant would not agree to see me. I was at a loss for the next step. I had never been on the base and had no contacts. I decided to write a letter to the commanding officer of the base, giving as few details as possible. I closed the letter with a request to meet with him. The appointment was granted.

At the meeting, I was told that the matter was closed, and if it were to be reopened, it would have to be done through the legal channels on the base, which meant a military tribunal would conduct the trial. At last we found a window opened to Collier, but he needed a good attorney to represent him. Having been out of work for a long time now, he did not have money for food, not to mention funds for an attorney. The only income for the household came by way of his wife's low-wage job. There was no money or provision in my budget for an attorney, either, nor was his union willing or able to help in this area.

Then I decided to do a dumb thing—I decided to represent Collier myself. I informed the officials at the base that Collier was willing to appeal his dismissal through the channels, and I had been given the power of attorney to represent him, not as a New Jersey lawyer licensed to practice law in the state, but as a legal representative of Collier. The date set for the trial was only three weeks away.

For what it was worth, I told Collier that I had been exposed to the legal profession as the first African-American admitted to the University of Missouri School of Law but had dropped out before the end of the first semester. Although that was some thirty-five years prior, my interest in law had not decreased. I was widely read on the subject and had completed a couple of correspondence courses on torts and contracts.

One thing I knew for sure: an adequate preparation was necessary for me to defend Collier. First, I researched every aspect of the marijuana substance. I needed to know its impact on the social user and on those who were labeled addicted. I wanted to know how widespread its use was in the state, how mind-altering it could be and under what circumstances. I wanted to study arrest records and the penalties for varying degrees of usage and possession. I was especially interested in usage by employees at

McGuire, and how other cases were handled. I investigated McGuire's military police—how many drivers they pulled over, reasons for stopping them, and how many were black and how many were white. What was the total population of workers on the base by race and by sex, and among those, who were most often arrested?

I wanted a copy of Collier's personnel files and some background on his supervising sergeant. I sought every piece of information I could think of that my brain could hold. I knew that I would not get everything I requested, but in logic, I could make a case for what was denied just as well as for what was present if I was astute enough.

Finally, I listed the witnesses that needed to be questioned. Unfortunately, Collier was a rather private person and did not have one strong character witness. The other side, however, had a number of witnesses lined up to testify against him.

Finally the day of the trial came. There I was, facing a hearing judge, who was a full colonel, and the base prosecuting attorney, who was a captain and a lawyer. Yes, I was nervous but could not let it be known because Collier's future was in my untrained and incapable hands. I took copious notes as the captain presented McGuire's case against Collier. He called on several witnesses, the first being the military policemen who ordered Collier to pull over. They stated what they allegedly found, and why he was arrested.

On cross-examination, I asked all sorts of questions, just trying to get a feel for what was happening. Most of my questions were objected to and upheld. This helped to get a feel for how to phrase my questions and when to probe further without giving rise to an objection that would be upheld. After two full days of trial, we came to our closing arguments.

McGuire's prosecutor stated in closing arguments that Collier had willfully violated the law by possessing an illegal substance, that the MPs were justified in pulling his car over because he was weaving on and off the road, and that the supervising sergeant was justified in dismissing Collier based on the facts of the case, his negative evaluations, and the statements of witnesses substantiating the integrity of those findings.

Now it was my turn. I pursued the argument along several points. One, Collier had worked a double shift because his replacement called in sick. There was no evidence that the replacement was sick, but there was evidence that he sometimes drank too much. After working sixteen hours, coming off a holiday, Collier was naturally tired. It was less than fifteen minutes between the time that Collier clocked out and the time he was stopped by the MPs. This was hardly enough time to consume more than one joint or, at the maximum, two if consumed in succession.

Even if such were the case, the prosecution did not prove that smoking two marijuana cigarettes would cause Collier to lose control of a vehicle. The MPs said that they found four rolled joints in a pouch, but they were never submitted for evidence. Only one was submitted. What happened to the other three?

Then there was the matter of the arrest. Why was it that the number of blacks pulled over was so much higher than the number of whites, when the latter group made up the larger portion of the workforce? Regarding the negative evaluation by the supervising sergeant, why was it that Collier and other blacks had suddenly begun to receive negative evaluations when previously they had received good reports? Why was it that the witnesses corroborating the position of the supervising sergeant were also his golf buddies and had no real contact with Collier? The judge said that he would render his decision the next morning. I knew that I had done my best; I knew that a real attorney could have done better, but I also knew that I had punched a few holes in the prosecution's case. But I was not quite ready for the verdict that came. Not only was Collier found not guilty, but the judge believed the MPs stopped him illegally.

He was reinstated in his former position with seniority to be credited as if he had never been dismissed. It was ordered that he be given back pay for all the time that he was off work, including any special pay that would have come because of holidays. All his benefits were to be made current, including vacation time lost. And then the bombshell: Collier was granted one full year under the supervising sergeant where there would be no opportunity to provide a single negative report on Collier.

The media gave full coverage to the results of this verdict and followed up to see that the verdict rendered was followed. Other African-Americans later came forth with complaints, but, to my understanding, they were handled satisfactorily without having to be adjudicated. This was a big day, not only for African-Americans, but also for Air Force Base. The positive change reverberated to the Fort Dix base, and both bases have been operating without many incidents since. There have even been African-American commanding officers since then. Perhaps the Collier case had an impact.

At least the word was out—this preacher was a rebel.

Community Housing Resources Board

THE BURLINGTON County Community Action Program (BCCAP) contacted me in 1979 through its housing counseling office regarding the housing problem in Willingboro. It seemed that HUD and other agencies were recommending more people to its office for mortgage counseling assistance from Willingboro than from any other municipality. They did not have adequate staff to handle all of the referrals. This became an immediate concern of mine since I was active in Willingboro. Although an exhaustive study was not conducted, it was determined from a limited sampling that a large number of people had either lost their homes or were in or near foreclosure. This was an alarming fact, one that demanded immediate attention.

Alpha Church decided that we would open an office where people could come for free counseling regarding how to best handle their finances before they got into real trouble with mortgage payments. This could be accomplished relatively easily by utilizing some people who had banking experience and were willing to donate some free time for this purpose. A couple of qualified people from the Alpha Church volunteered. However, we discovered that this was not what people needed the most. Without exception, those who came were already in trouble with their mortgages, and they were African-Americans.

The people who had been recruited to deal with budgeting, before a financial crisis was reached, were not equipped to deal with this. What we needed were HUD-certified housing counselors who would be recognized by the lending institutions that held the mortgages.

We made the contact with HUD and discovered that a training session would be starting soon. Before we would be allowed to send people for training, we would have to create a Community Housing Resources Board. A representative of HUD, who was stationed in the Federal Building in Camden, walked us through the steps.

There were a number of reasons they fell behind in their mortgage payments: loss of job, transportation problems, tax increases. Others made the mistake of over-extending themselves by adding new maintenance-free siding to their home, new furniture, new vehicles, clothing, etc. Some of the reasons were legitimate, while others were not. The fact was that many people were from three months to more than a year behind in their mortgage payments.

Steven Swartz, an attorney with the public defender's office (as best I remember), joined the board and did most of the legal work. Now that we were established, we needed funding to get at least a secretary and a full-time counselor.

Although we were called the Community Housing Resources Board, we knew that most of our cases would probably be coming from Willingboro, as we took that portion of the caseload that normally went to BCCAP.

Willingboro was having most of the problems; therefore, it seemed appropriate that we approach the township council about possible funding. The first time around we did not even get on the agenda, and we never did find out why, although we had some suspicions that we shall turn to later. This matter was as serious as any we had confronted and should not be left to die, not only because of the amount of work that we had done, but also because of the tremendous need in Willingboro. People who lost their homes had lost the most important asset they had, and it was a demoralizing experience. We turned next to the county. With very few questions asked and absolutely no resistance at the time, we received funding for a secretary, a counselor, and office rent.

We located the office in Burlington City in the building where Steven Swartz had his office. We were now in business. We had an excellent board of trustees including Dorothy Riley, a veteran African-American politician who passed away in early 1999. She represented Palmyra-Cinnaminson, and other members were from different areas of the county. The two full-time staff persons were white. Not that this made a difference to me, but the selection process was a bit shady, as it was later discovered.

A caseload was built up rapidly, and a number of people who would have otherwise lost their homes were spared that crisis by the intervention *efforts* of CHURB. As was expected, most of the cases came from Willingboro, so in effect CHURB became Willingboro's program, paid for by the county. I let this be known whenever possible.

When we had our monthly meeting, the full-time counselor gave a report. I raised some concern that the intake of cases was really on the increase, but the number of cases actually discharged was decreasing. The counselor explained that cases were taking more time than normal. We accepted this reply because we had no evidence to the contrary. Later, a client approached me with an allegation that the counselor was prejudiced against blacks and did not really try to help them the way she should. Thus one Saturday when the office was closed, I went through some records. I was chairman of the board and had full authority to review files and gain complete knowledge of client counseling. It was not difficult to conclude that the counselor had deliberately held up cases that should have been closed and placed into the post-counseling file. I spoke to her about it quietly. She went to Steven Swartz, who supported her and accused me of meddling with her work. She then resigned without the contractual notice of two weeks and went to the unemployment office and applied for unemployment compensation, saying that she was forced to quit because the board and its chairman were harassing her. I denied the charge and went for the scheduled hearing.

To my surprise, the inspector had already determined that she was correct and nothing that I said would change his mind. However, he advised me that his decision could be appealed for an administrative hearing. I felt certain that justice would prevail there since people who were not in any way involved would be hearing the case. Was I in for a rude awakening. It was told to me, in no uncertain terms, that it was difficult to understand how the counselor had been able to stay as long as she did.

"You people," the counselor said during the administrative hearing, "would force anyone to leave."

This was my first introduction to the New Jersey Unemployment Office on High Street, and it was the last in that case since we lost.

This episode taught CHURB and me a lesson about the politics of selective humanity, where truth often has nothing to do with justice, especially in its denial. We were dealing with a structure that was supported by our tax dollars, but controlled by white society. The people in ultimate authority were concerned about keeping the control of power in their hands. One of the ways to maintain power in a situation like this is to hide the mistakes made in the way things were handled. Had they admitted that the counselor had been in error, they would have had to deny her the benefit of unemployment checks. That would have meant denying one of their own. But that was only one issue.

Another issue is this: in admitting she was wrong, they would also be admitting that we were correct. Then, she would either have to return to work or not receive any benefits. In the first instance, it would have been impossible since we knew that she was not treating the clients fairly. In the second instance, they would have had to deal with the possibility that we would spread the word that she was a racist who had done harm to blacks intentionally and may have even caused some to lose their homes. If right had prevailed, then the word may have reached the press. We also drew the conclusion that if justice were denied at the level of an administrative hearing, then the situation must have been even worse at the point of initial contact when blacks and whites were competing for the same jobs. Justice may also have been denied when blacks applied for unemployment benefits. If that much discretion were allowed at the level that we were operating, and we were the employer, who was there to speak for the unemployed? It was a terrible indictment upon that office and upon the state, but we were not able to tell the story at the time.

Steven Swartz quit the board after that, and the Board of Chosen Freeholders of Burlington County did not renew the contract for the program, which again shows how the members of white society protect each other, which is a lesson that African-Americans need to learn. Learning this lesson and practicing it will put our diverse society in a better position for future progress.

After this counselor left, we hired another person who had completed law school and was preparing for his exam. The office was moved to Willingboro to a space provided rent-free by the Alpha Baptist Church of Christ Nurturing Center, Inc. The new counselor did not work out at all. He simply was too lazy to do the work. Instead he spent more time in the office than out with clients. The next person hired was a lady who had been a housing counselor for Urban League in Camden.

Since we were just about out of funds, we decided to appeal to the Willingboro Township Council once again.

It was the appearance before the Willingboro Township Council that brought me into direct contact with Frank Quinn for the first time since I had left Rotary, about five years prior. I introduced myself to council; of course everyone already knew me. I requested permission to present our staff counselor and requested permission to let her explain the program. Council listened to her, and I do not believe that there was a person on council who could not see that this was one of the best, if not the best, programs that the council had been asked to support. At that time, we had about 350 families needing help with their mortgages. Our program had proven its worth, and without it many people would lose their homes.

Instead of council asking more details regarding the budget, staffing, demographic data, etc., they seemed more interested in what Frank Quinn had to say. Quinn asked questions of me regarding my ordination, education and the qualifications I had for the job of housing counselor. He knew, as did every member of council, that his line of questions were irrelevant. I was not seeking a job or a position for myself. I was there on behalf of CHURB. After my objections to being harassed by Quinn, Mayor Marie Bell finally intervened and advised Quinn that his questions were out of line and that his comments should be directed toward the issue.

It was evident that although five years had passed since my departure from Rotary, the anger that Frank Quinn had with my raising the question about the report of the nominating committee was still very much alive. We did not get a second hearing on the grant request.

The work of the Community Housing Resources Board continued for a couple of more years, being staffed by members of Alpha Baptist Church. Even to this day, we still will intervene for a few people as time permits.

At the request of HUD, CHURB, at its height, sought to get the Burlington County Board of Realtors to sign a covenant saying that they would not discriminate in showing houses to prospective buyers based on race or religion. But the board would not even consider it for a vote. After pressuring them for an up or down vote, they put it before the group and the vote, we were told, was a unanimous and resounding NO.

We then approached some individual realtors that we knew personally, and, to our surprise and dismay, they would not sign such a covenant either. They felt that if they signed a covenant not to discriminate that it would be published and that would frighten away their white clients. They were correct that it would be published, and they may have been correct that some white clients would have been frightened away.

But the strange part about the turn of events was that a non-discriminatory policy had been on the book for years in New Jersey, and if they had signed it, it would have only been saying that they were willing to comply with the law. Even when it was explained to them this way, they still would not sign. We had to conclude that Burlington County, even as late as 1982, had such strong racist attitudes that even those realtors who made money from blacks as well as whites were afraid to break rank.

Today, realtors will hire black agents because they know that they make good salespersons when the potential buyer is also black. However, until we see on the bottom of the realtor's ad, "Equal Opportunity Seller," we cannot even begin to think that the practice of racial steering is a thing of the past or even on its way out.

The Nathaniel Evans, M.D., Controversy

NATHANIEL EVANS, M.D., an African-American, began practice at the Zurbrugg Memorial Hospital in 1979 as a part-time staff physician. Within a span of only four years, Evans became director of Emergency Medicine at both Zurbrugg hospitals, the Rancocas Valley and Riverside divisions. Under Dr. Evans' directorship, admissions were boosted, and community relations and continuing education for staff became top priorities. Those with whom Dr. Evans worked described him as a passionate, skillful, and compassionate physician.

I can attest personally to both his compassion and his skills. I first met Dr. Evans when he visited a worship service at the original site of the Alpha Baptist Church at 175 Somerset Drive in Willingboro. I had fainted during the presentation of a sermon, just before the invitation to Christian discipleship was extended to the congregation. Some members of the congregation helped me upstairs, where they sat me in a comfortable chair. To our surprise and delight, Dr. Evans was in the audience that morning and observed what happened and followed those assisting me. Once upstairs, he examined me and concluded that I was simply suffering from a period of overexertion, which could be cured completely by a little rest. He was absolutely correct; I rested and I was fine. He had responded as a doctor and a compassionate person. Since no one knew him, he could have left me to the attention of the members of the church, but his commitment to the practice of emergency medicine and to his faith would not allow him to do that.

In January of 1985, an announcement was made that the expiration of Dr. Nathaniel Evans' contract as provider of emergency room services at both divisions of Zurbrugg Memorial Hospital would take effect in June of that year. The Zurbrugg Memorial Hospital Board of Directors put out for bids the operation of the emergency room services. According to published reports, the Rancocas Valley division executive committee as well as the medical staff gave both support of and confidence in Dr. Evans and passed motions declaring their unified support of the retention of what had now become known as Dr. Evans' emergency room group. Precisely because Dr. Evans and his team had such an unblemished record of serving the patients who came to the hospital for emergency care, they became the unqualified favorite of the medical staffs and, to an extent, the larger Willingboro community.

However, on April 30, 1985, the Rancocas Valley executive committee met to deliberate and decide on a new contract for farming out the emergency room services. It was during this meeting that the announcement was made that a contract had been signed with an emergency group out of Woodbury, New Jersey. This group was led by Dr. James George and was referred to as the EPA group. The new contract, which Evans had lost, became effective as of midnight September 1, 1985.

During their announcement of the awarding of the contract to the EPA group led by Dr. James George, the hospital officials took great pains in making it clear that the choice was made strictly on the matter of finance. In short, the contract dealt with the bottom line, which was dollars, and it did not in any way reflect upon the quality of care that had been offered by the Evans' Group over the years, which had been of a superior quality. It was indicated, in the announcement that was made public, that the selection of the EPA Group could save the Zurbrugg Memorial Hospital, over a two-year period, funds in the range of $123,000. To many people in the larger community, especially in Willingboro, it seemed that both Dr. Evans' group's track record as the medical provider and the medical staff recommendation that he be retained as the director of Emergency Room Services by the Zurbrugg Memorial Hospital administration and the board of directors were completely ignored. The tendency to ignore medical staff recommendations was seen as the actual kiss of death to Dr. Evans' group's chances of gaining a contract renewal.

According to some of the reports that were being published in the media, some physicians questioned whether the hospital was following its own bylaws in evaluating the bids that were submitted. Reportedly, they also questioned whether the board of directors was fully apprised of all the details of the matter before they cast their vote to select Dr. George over Dr. Evans.

While this doubt loomed large within the medical staff of the hospital, the whole idea of Dr. Evans' departure from the position as the Director of the Emergency Room Services spurred other physicians and emergency squad members to rally their support of the Evans group. This widespread support for Dr. Evans put the whole scenario into greater public focus and engendered a rather large amount of negative publicity for the hospital. Naturally, the hospital administrators became very uncomfortable because they knew that they had been very careful to explain to the public why the decision had been made to award the contract to the George group. They were confident that they had done it in a way such that people would understand that the decision was a matter of finance and maintenance of quality and not in any way related to race.

However, the administrators now knew that the process was not going the way they had planned. The nonrenewal of the contract with the Evans' group had evolved into a controversy, which not only sparked an unprecedented response in the black community, but literally opened a Pandora's box. It also resulted in a short-term breakdown in the relationship between the medical staff and the Zurbrugg Memorial Hospital board and administrators, as it was later reported.

In addition to this, there was a continuing kind of public denunciation of the Zurbrugg Memorial Hospital administration, which received wide publicity.

In an effort to try to reverse the negative publicity that was being generated by the Evans controversy, the hospital made the decision to hold a public information meeting in order that opinions could be expressed. Many Willingboro residents and community leaders attended the meeting. However, the meeting did not generate the kind of closure that was anticipated; instead, the meeting created more outrage among the members of the community, especially among African-Americans who were keeping track of the controversy. It prompted some who were at the meeting to say publicly that *they* would encourage future patients to try to avoid the Zurbrugg Memorial Hospital and seek other hospitals as a way of protesting the handling of the Evans controversy. One of the reasons, perhaps, that this generated so much publicity and encouraged widespread community response from the African-American sector of Willingboro was because Dr. Evans was the first and only African-American physician during this period who was working full-time as a local physician.

Sequentially, Dr. Evans filed a suit against the Zurbrugg Memorial Hospital alleging that there was a breach of contract, unfair treatment, and even racial discrimination against him. This suit provoked the Zurbrugg Memorial Hospital into filing a countersuit against Evans, and, in order to cover all bases, an additional all-inclusive suit against what were referred to as "anonymous" John and Jane Doe citizens who were supportive of Evans.

Persons who were supportive of the efforts to retain Dr. Evans and his group as head of the emergency room at the hospital picketed the hospital for more than a week before the scheduled transition from the Evans group to the George group was to take place. Among the signs carried by those who were picketing was a *sign* that was kind of a novel read; taken straight out of Hollywood's Death Valley days. It read, "Will Death Valley days return to Willingboro?" Some observers have suggested that this particular language on a sign, perhaps more than anything else in the entire saga of the Willingboro/Evans controversy, was the thing that killed it for Dr. Evans. They considered this sign as sending a very negative message to the community and could even have been libelous. At any rate, it caused many people who were supportive of Dr. Evans' group within the medical arena to withdraw such support and terminate their support of Dr. Evans.

It is ironic how this one particular sign had so many overtures to it that allowed people to interpret it from many different perspectives. One such interpretation, which would seem to have caught on very intensely among many persons, particularly white persons who were not familiar or did not relish the idea of pickets, suggested that Dr. Evans himself was a person who stood in the gap between Death Valley days and quality care at the hospital. This, of course, cast a very negative shadow on those who saw the *sign* or who heard about the *sign* and thought in this mind-set. It also shows, with unquestionable clarity, how even one phrase can have such a tremendous impact. The question will never be answered but I have to raise it anyway. Had this *sign* not been carried by those picketing, would Dr. Evans have been successful in winning and overturning the contract that had been awarded to the George group? Those who would say yes must also believe that the minority people were responsible for preventing the Evans group from being reinstated as the holder of the contract with the Zurbrugg Hospital, since they were the most vocal in demanding the change. For others who did not believe that a single *sign* could have that much impact, it was not the sign that made the difference; rather it was racism that prevented the Evans group from regaining its position as head of the emergency room services.

However, there will always be that large segment of people who did not place as much emphasis upon the sign in any way at all but looked at the bottom line and felt that it was a financial matter. There is still another point to be considered. In any kind of protest movement, there may be signs that are literally damning to the cause, while others speak to the real issue. This is an historical fact and is not likely to change. After all, it is not the message on the sign that makes the difference; it is the language at the bargaining table that does. All the signs are meant to do is show the urgency of going to the table to talk responsibly. However, we cannot suspend reality, and supporters of just causes must consider all of these factors when creating and carrying the signs because we have not yet removed the cause for occasional picketing in the first place. African-Americans must be careful in how they endorse such actions that may turn off the support of positive-thinking whites, because they need those kinds of people in the white community to help create the new community where actions are taken based on true justice and not determined by each situation and its participants.

However, Dr. Evans later filed an injunction to keep the George group from taking over the emergency room services on September 1, 1985. But the Superior Court judge denied the appeal and the transition did take place as scheduled on September 1, 1985. As of this writing Dr. Evans currently has what appears to be a substantial practice with offices located on Beverly Rancocas Road in Willingboro. He is affiliated with the Memorial Hospital in Burlington County, which is located in Mt. Holly, New Jersey. His patients, one would suspect because of location, are primarily Willingboro residents and are referred to the Memorial Hospital when hospitalization is needed or when outpatient services are needed.

Questions: Did the boycott by Dr. Evans' supporters have any real value? Did the boycott reach its goal? Was this action a loss to the hospital, Dr. Evans, or the African-American community? One could not answer these questions with certainty because the Zurbrugg Memorial Hospital has gone through many changes since the time of the Evans group. There was a period when it lost tremendous amounts of money, far more than the $123,000 that it saved over a two-year period in the contract with the George group. It even designed and built a new emergency room, which looms larger than the medical staff that services it. I say that because I was present at the dedication of the new addition and did not hear any mention of the medical team that was contracted to render service through it.

However, as of this writing, the former Zurbrugg Hospital is now owned by the Lourdes Hospital and will become a Catholic hospital when all medical procedures associated with abortions are discontinued. Today, there are only four administrators at the Rancocas Hospital, all of them white, and this represents a sealing down of the administrators' staff. In an interview with one of the administrators in connection with this story, I was informed that under the Lourdes banner, the hospital will be operated in a way that all hospitals should be operated, without regard to race or gender when it comes to employment and service, and that is a good thing. It is up to the African-Americans and the management team at the hospital to make this a practice that will carry over into the next century. For the residents of Willingboro who need hospitalization, it is far more convenient to travel to the facility in Willingboro than it is to other hospitals in nearby areas, and this fact must be placed above any personal concerns of any medical professional who may be establishing staff relations with a hospital. An equal opportunity employer means little unless prospective employees seek employment there. This is as much true of a hospital as it is of any other corporate structure. African-American patients should inform their doctors where they prefer to go when they need hospitalization, and this will ultimately impact where those doctors seek staff relationships. This could also serve to attract more African-American physicians to the hospital, which is closest to where their patients live.

New Jersey's First Black Correctional Facility Chief

NEW JERSEY MADE history and so did Ronald M. Grooms when he was chosen as the first black person to be appointed as super-intendent of Leesburg State Prison in February of 1983. Grooms had previously served as assistant superintendent of Rahway State Prison, the facility where the movie *Scared Straight* was filmed.

Grooms' tenure in the correction system began in 1955. Before assuming the top-level position at Leesburg, Grooms spent several years working at the Johnstone Training and Research Center and as a senior inspector at the Skillman Training School for Boys.

Sidney Hicks, another African-American, served for several years during the 1980s as the superintendent of what was then known as Bordentown Correctional Facility. Under his administration, a number of innovations were implemented. These included an improved food service program and extensive vocational and rehabilitative opportunities for all inmates. He left his position for another position with the state.

The appointments of Grooms and Hicks did not occur until ten years after a major complaint of racism and abuse was reviewed by the Commission of Civil Rights. The review occurred after three mysterious deaths of inmates in Trenton State Prison. Many African-Americans believe that it was not until James Florio became governor that black inmates began to feel that someone really cared about them.

In talking to a number of correctional officers in preparation for this study, the feeling is that the new commissioner of the system, Jack Tehune, is more intent on building jails than on any program that will curb the high rate of recidivism.

A number of African-Americans have served as assistant superintendents over the years, and several hold high-ranking offices today in a system that is over 80 percent minority.

Search for Chaplain for Rancocas Hospital

ONE MORNING in the spring of 1990, I received a call from the office of the director of volunteers at the Rancocas Hospital inviting me to be part of an advisory committee to the chief administrative officer of the hospital. I was told that I would be one of several ministers who would be asked to serve on this new committee. Once in place, the group would fulfill an important function for the hospital and the community. After learning that we would not be meeting more than once per month and may not meet every month, I agreed to serve.

The first meeting was held a couple of weeks later in the hospital's administrative conference room at 11:00 a.m. and concluded with a lunch served by the hospital. This was mostly a get-acquainted meeting where all of us had an opportunity to introduce ourselves and meet the director of volunteer services and the chief administrator of the hospital. About a dozen people attended the meeting – three African-Americans, the remainder, white.

When the introductions were over, the chief administrator thanked all of us for coming and for our willingness to serve on the advisory committee and told us why we were there. He indicated that his desire was to have the hospital become more closely related to the communities it served, and he could think of no better channel to help establish this relationship than through the pastors. He assured us that he and the entire administrative staff of the hospital were there to assist the pastors in any way they could and that any suggestions that we had would be given priority consideration.

We discussed issues of parking for the clergy, which was a problem, identification badges, and more freedom of movement within the hospital. All of these areas were addressed to our satisfaction.

The question was raised regarding the powers of the advisory committee and we were told that we would not have any voting powers, but our suggestions and concerns would be relayed to the board of directors with the full power of his office behind them. Someone asked why he needed an advisory committee if he had a board of directors and how he would distinguish between the two, other than by the absence of the power of one to vote. The response was that the board of directors was comprised of a broad-based representation from the community and had the final say regarding the policies of the hospital but the advisory group would be able to suggest ideas that would lead to the generation of policy by the board. The committee would also be able to let him know the pulse of the people in the community, and his office could respond to the community's concerns without the need for a policy decision from the board of directors.

I listened to what was being said by the administrator and, judging from the response of the guests, it was obvious that he was having a positive impact upon the group. As much as I desired to see this committee organized and functioning in ways that would be of benefit to the hospital, the constituencies we served, and the larger communities we represented, I had a concern regarding the composition of the board of directors that had been on my mind for a long time before this meeting. I asked if there were any minorities on the board of directors of the hospital and was told that there weren't any at the present time but that could change in the future. This gave me the window that I needed to raise the next question in a straightforward manner. I asked if it were true that there were no blacks on the board of directors because an endowment was given to the hospital by an individual with the stipulation that no black persons would ever serve on the board of directors. There was complete silence and an absence of movement in the room as we waited for the administrator's response to the question. He responded that I was correct but that donor's feelings did not reflect the current thinking of the hospital administration, which was being demonstrated by bringing us together as his advisory group. I suggested that being in an advisory position to the administration was not the same as being in a position to effect policy. He admitted that it was not the same but reiterated his stance that we would have substantial influence on the board of directors through him.

When I saw that the white pastors were shocked by this disclosure regarding membership on the board of directors, I suggested that one way to demonstrate his commitment toward making the advisory committee a group with an effective voice would be to take our suggestion to integrate the board of directors, even if it meant the loss of revenue from this dead contributor. At this point, a black pastor stood up and said that he did not want to serve on a committee where someone would be speaking to him from the grave.

I knew that I had opened a Pandora's box, and the best way out of this would be to give the administrator some time to digest what he had heard, which must have been a surprise to him. I suggested that I felt the group would be willing to work with him as advisors as long as our counsel was taken seriously and we could see evidence of the same. I also requested that he keep us informed on the progress that was being made on the board issue. We thanked the administrator for the invitation to serve on the advisory committee and felt that our partnering together could become increasingly beneficial to all concerned as we worked cooperatively in the future. A time for the next meeting was set, and we had lunch and left.

The director of volunteers hosted all of the subsequent meetings that we had and the chief administrator attended occasionally and stayed for a brief period of time. At one meeting, the advisory committee was asked to assist in the process of selecting a chaplain for the hospital. We wanted to know what our role would be and how much influence we would have in the final selection of the candidate. It was made clear to us that we would interview all of the candidates, and the person chosen would be based upon our recommendations, which was pleasing to hear. The announcement of the position had wide exposure, and applications came from a wide area of the country.

Since this was a function given over to the committee, with the director of volunteers servicing as staff, we elected one of our members to chair the group. We reviewed the applications and rated them. Some we designated for an interview and others were simply filed.

While the interview process was being conducted, a *lady clergy friend* of mine from Cleveland, Ohio, arrived for her annual stay as my family's house-guest This was her retreat from the big city. I shared with her the information regarding the committee's efforts in trying to find a qualified candidate to recommend as the first full-time chaplain for the hospital. To my **amazement**, she said that she might be interested. I asked *her* if she had a resume with her, and she said that she did not but could write one if we made a typewriter available to her, which we did. When I read her resume, I knew it would impress the committee. Our guest was a registered nurse with a specialty in geriatric nursing, director of nursing, a clergywoman, a seminary graduate, youth and choir director in her church, a well-known community activist, a nationally-known singer, and had previously served as a chaplain. She was willing to move to this area for a position even if it paid less money than she was earning because she wanted to do ministry in a more personal way than she was able to do in the large hospitals in Cleveland. She also liked our community and had come here annually for several years now. When I gave a copy of my friend's resume to the director of volunteers, I was sure that an invitation for an interview would be extended.

The first response was that she was **overqualified** for the job. I was not going to accept that because it had been used as an excuse in too many instances to keep blacks out of certain positions. When a company did not want to hire a black they would say one of two things–the candidate was either underqualified or overqualified. The result was always the same, nonselected by the company. I strongly recommended that she be given an interview and then let the committee make the decision. I was then told that they had spent all of the budget allowed for travel for candidates from outside of the area, to which I responded that the person in question was a guest in our home as we spoke. She promised to get back to me but never did.

My friend returned to Cleveland but I still thought the matter was worth pursuing, so I raised the question again. This time I was told that an *effort* had been made to contact the potential applicant at her home and there was no response, so the director of volunteers concluded that the interest was no longer present, on the part of my friend. I asked why she had waited so long to contact her and why she did not make the effort while my friend was a guest in my home. So I called my friend and was told what I suspected, that no contact had been made with her and that she was still interested but not desperate because she had a secure job. I reported to the director of volunteers that my friend was still interested and would pay her own way for the interview if need be. She said good, but not a word was ever mentioned to the committee about her becoming a candidate, and I did not want to bring it before them as it would be a deviation from our practice and also create a hostile environment in which to work. I separated myself from the matter, fully convinced that the time was not right to have a black person serve as a chaplain at the Rancocas Hospital, any more than it was ready to have a black serve on the board of directors.

The chair of the committee resigned the position due to the impending change of leadership at his church and suggested my name as a replacement, which was accepted by the group. He agreed to continue to participate as much as possible. In the meantime, the Rancocas Hospital in Willingboro and the Zurbrugg Memorial Hospital in Riverside, New Jersey, began to partner together but with separate administrators. The Riverside division had its own advisory committee, which was under the leadership of its chaplain and of which I was a part.

The advertised position for a chaplain was reduced from that of full-time to one of part-time services at both hospitals, Rancocas and Zurbrugg Memorial Hospital in Riverside, New Jersey. And both secured part-time persons to serve in these positions.

The ownership of the hospital kept changing and that brought in new leadership with each change and, gradually, I lost interest in the project and resigned. With my resignation, the committee faded away, and we reverted to serving our former roles of ministering to members of our own congregation. Additionally, some of us have our names on the part-time chaplains list of rotating clergy who can be called on an emergency basis.

I understand that a black person was quietly brought onto the board of directors of Rancocas, but that is all history now as the new owner, Lourdes, does not have a board of directors at the hospital. In an interview with one of the four hospital administrators, I was assured that when the time comes for a board of directors to be established, its composition will be reflective of the population it serves, which means that at least 25 percent of the board members will be African-American, and I believe him.

Second Black News Journal Targets Willingboro

THE *Black Suburban Journal* was introduced into the Delaware Valley in 1997, becoming only the second newspaper to target the African-American population of Willingboro. Of course, there have been a number of one- or two-page typed handouts with limited distribution, and for a while, the *Philadelphia Tribune*, one of the oldest black newspapers in the country, enjoyed a very limited exposure in Willingboro. In the early 1980s, the *Burlington County Black Journal* began a weekly publication that was distributed throughout the county but primarily targeted Willingboro.

By the time I was introduced to the *Burlington County Black Journal* and was asked to become its editor, there was a weekly circulation of 5,000, excluding the bulk drop to selected cities around the county. Within a few months, the production had grown to 12,000. It was basically a free paper, but enjoyed nearly 1,000 paid subscriptions during its peak.

Although the paper was tabloid in size, it was a rather high-quality production that covered most of the local news of Willingboro and the surrounding areas and carried some national stories of interest to black people. It was nonpartisan in its political view and non-racist in its philosophical view. Stories that were barely mentioned in the *Burlington County Times* or were only given a few lines were given full coverage in the *BCBJ*, if they impacted the black community.

At one point, the paper was being distributed to 90 percent of the homes in Willingboro, and there were no noticeable objections from the white community that they did not want to receive it on their lawns. Even a few guest editorials that were published in the *BCBJ* were written by white people.

The paper really should have succeeded because it had a strong potential market and the advertisements were sufficient to carry the production and most of the distribution costs.

Three obstacles caused the demise of the paper. First, it was discovered that the publisher, who was on the scene when I arrived, was a fraud and had been utilizing false credentials. We learned further that some of the stories that he claimed to have written were boilerplates that were given for free with a membership in the *National Black News Network*. Added to this discovery, it was learned that the publisher was staying at Howard Johnson's on 541 and had run up an enormous bill that he could not afford to pay. Even if we took his salary for several months, it would not be sufficient. We paid the debt to Howard Johnson's and sent him on his way.

The next obstacle was harder to overcome. It had to do with distribution. We found out that the young people we hired to deliver the papers were throwing them down the catch basin on the streets in front of houses and into free-standing dumpsters wherever they could be found and then claiming that the papers had been delivered. It was sad but true; we were paying them more per paper delivered than the *BCT* paid their deliverers, and yet nothing of this kind ever happened to the *BCT* papers scheduled for delivery (as far as we were able to determine).

We received numerous calls saying that the paper had not been received. We tried to respond to as many of the calls as possible, whether they were subscribers or not, but we fell short of our goal of a paper to every home.

The third hurdle that we faced was the one that caused us to be put out of business. The cost of production went up, and we lost some advertisers. We did not have a staff that was willing to solicit new advertisers. Silas Ricks, who was the major financier for the paper, and Lawrence Young, the second publisher, were the major sources of funding when the paper began to suffer financially. I contributed my time, which was quite a lot since as editor-in-chief, I laid out the whole paper. In fact, Ricks and Young had deceived me regarding the original publisher, and they also stated that there was ample revenue to keep the paper going during the lean period.

However, when all of the above events occurred and I was required to put in money, but was not paid any salary as promised and contracted, I knew it was time for me to step down. It was a difficult decision to make because it meant closing down the paper. It simply could not be maintained as a viable enterprise. When I stepped down, the paper went belly-up. I took Young and Ricks to court to try and recover some of the funds owed to me. I received a judgment against them, but was never able to collect any money.

Once again, because of deception, mismanagement, and lack of cooperation, another possible way to help the black people in Willingboro become a more vital part of the community was lost.

I had almost completely forgotten about the *Burlington County Black Journal* until the publisher of the *Black Suburban Journal* came to my office in 1997 and brought me a copy of his paper. He shared with me his dream for this new paper. I invited him to the meeting of the Willingboro Clergy Association, where he made his appeal for support of the paper.

In one of the latest editions of the *BSJ* there was an appeal to the people of Willingboro to support the paper by taking out subscriptions. The publisher indicated that over the short time that the paper had been published, over 500,000 copies were donated to this area.

I have read every issue of the paper and find that many articles in the paper make good reading material for any audience, while the remainder of the paper has a black readership in mind. The goal of the *BSJ* is to obtain 2,000 new paid subscriptions. This assumes a very small paid subscription base at present, which makes the goal quite achievable, when one considers that Willingboro is a community of roughly 40,000 residents with some 70 percent of them being black, according to the numbers published in the *BSJ*.

The publisher also plans to donate a portion of the profits to community groups that help promote the paper. Perhaps with that added incentive the *BSJ* will be successful.

As this treatise is being written, there remains one more opportunity to have a local paper that prints news that the majority of the people in Willingboro can use. What will happen? Will it succeed or will it fail? It seems as though once again, the answer is in the hands of the citizens of Willingboro.

Emergency Services

WHEN ONE IS ASKED to advocate for justice in the kind of society that has characterized the latter half of the twentieth century, a society torn by the racial divide, devastated by a lopsided economic table, disturbed by cries for change, fragmented by political allegiances and demagoguery, and weakened by the lessening influence of organized religion, it is expected that a positive response to become involved will always be challenging and often frustrating. If this person who is sought out for assistance is at the same time a religious leader who seeks the Christian way of justice, then the problem of making the decision borders on double jeopardy.

The Christian advocate for justice must respond to the alleged victim of injustice with two constant variables confronting him, both from the Bible: "Watch out for false prophets. They come to you in sheep's clothing, but inwardly they are ferocious wolves" (Matthew 7:15), and, "Do not forget to entertain strangers for by so doing some people have entertained angels without knowing it" (Hebrews 13:2). Herein lies the mystery, for the advocate for biblical justice could be damned if he does get involved with a stranger's request and damned if he doesn't.

Such has been my plight for most of my life, and such was the case when Patricia Jalpert (not her real name) came to my office in 1997 seeking my assistance, as pastor of the Alpha Church and a known advocate for justice. Although I had no prior relationship with her, I am a pastor and an advocate for justice, and here was a virtual stranger asking me to intervene in her fight for justice. Given the biblical mandate under which I exercise my calling to ministry, I said yes, with the references mentioned above notwithstanding.

Ms. Jalpert alleged that she had been forced to leave her position at Emergency Services because, as a Christian, she could no longer endure the serious breaches of ethics, morality, regulations of funding sources, abuse of consumers, misappropriation of funds, and falsification of statistical data to gain more funds than to which the agency was entitled. She alleged that all of this was taking place at Emergency Services, an agency that was headed by Nina Penta (not her real name), a colleague of mine and a person whom I highly respected.

My initial response was that I did not want to get involved because Ms. Penta had been a colleague for years and we had worked together on at least one major project and shared conversations on others. Not only that, but I did not believe that Ms. Penta could possibly have been guilty of all the allegations that were being leveled against her, and I told Ms. Jalpert as much. I knew that someone was in the wrong but that it could not have been Ms. Penta. With that thought, I was ready to show Ms. Jalpert to the door, when she said that there were many other people who would support her story. When asked if she had tried talking to Ms. Penta about the allegations she informed me that she had tried and that it would be useless trying to approach someone who was above Ms. Penta because they would never believe her. I could understand that because I did not believe her either.

The next day Ms. Jalpert returned with a white colleague who said that she used to work at Emergency Services and indicated that everything that Ms. Jalpert had said was true. I was also presented with a written statement concerning the allegations through these the two persons, but that was not enough to convince me to get involved. Together, they related many horrible stories, often interrupted by periods of seemingly uncontrollable tears, regarding the alleged wrongdoing within the agency. Seeing that this was not enough to convince me to get involved, they then volunteered to take a polygraph test to further convince me that they were telling the truth. Since Ms. Jalpert was going to pay for the test I did not see any harm in letting her spend her money, although I would not personally use the polygraph as the final test of truth; I prefer the statements from informed and unbiased witnesses instead. The tests were administered and the results indicated that they were telling the truth as far as the questions that were asked. I did not think that they were asked enough specific questions regarding the allegations but was informed that if too many details were asked, it would corrupt the results of the test, but those that were asked were sufficient to support the integrity of their responses.

After the tests were over, I asked them what they wanted to see happen. Ms. Jalpert wanted to see Ms. Penta fired because she was the one who led the agency, knew what was going on in the agency, and had responsibility for every wrong thing that was happening there. Ms. Jalpert's friend simply wanted to support Ms. Jalpert in whatever she wanted. She made the point of how close she was to Ms. Jalpert and would do anything to help her in whatever she wanted to accomplish.

Based upon the information that I had—statements of two witnesses, the extensive written narrative written by her friend who was one of the witnesses, and the results of the polygraph tests—I reluctantly agreed to look into the matter. First I contacted two agency CEOs whom I respected and thought would be in a position to know the facts concerning at least some of Ms. Jalpert's allegations. Their responses neither confirmed nor denied Ms. Jalpert's story. Both of them knew that I felt duty-bound to follow through with my inquiry to the next level, which was the Trenton Diocese Office of Catholic Charities in Trenton. I knew that once I contacted Trenton, the matter would no longer be restricted to just a couple of people, and that made me uncomfortable, but it was something that I had to do anyway. I wrote a letter to the executive director of Catholic Charities who responded immediately with a promise to look into the matter.

Within a week I received a telephone call from the executive director who made an appointment to come down to my office with the purpose of sharing with me the results of their investigation of Ms. Jalpert's allegations. During the session, I was informed that a thorough investigation of Ms. Jalpert's allegations had been conducted over a period of three days by persons from the Trenton office.

The results were very straightforward: they had discovered some inappropriate behavior at the agency and some management problems and had instituted some stringent measures that would ensure that the agency would be run effectively in the future. However, he said that they did not discover anything of a criminal nature at the agency as had been alleged by Ms. Jalpert. I asked him about the possibility of transferring Ms. Penta to another agency since the management problems occurred under her watch. He was more inclined to watch over her than to remove her from the position of head of Emergency Services. It was a little less than I had requested but it was more than would have been done without my intervention.

When I shared with Ms. Jalpert the results of my meeting with the representative from Trenton, she became irate and began shouting that they were all in the cover-up together. I tried to calm her down and requested that she give it a chance to work; after all, something had been accomplished, although not as much as we sought. She did not feel that anything had been accomplished and said that she was going to take her case to the Burlington County prosecuting attorney's office, which she did. The detective from the prosecuting attorney's office who was assigned the case knew that I was involved in the matter and, by this time, so did some other people in the county.

After several weeks passed, Ms. Jalpert came into my office with the information that Ms. Penta had been terminated from her position at Emergency Services and escorted from the building. I asked her for the source of her information and how she knew it was correct. I was somewhat disappointed because all I had wanted was for Ms. Penta to be transferred to another agency and not terminated, and I thought that Ms. Jalpert would be quite satisfied with what she had helped to accomplish. I was not quite ready for the complete removal of Ms. Penta.

Ms. Jalpert responded that she would not be satisfied until everyone in the agency was removed and the agency closed down because it had been so infiltrated with the "powers of evil" brought on by Ms. Penta. I knew that Ms. Jalpert was asking for too much and felt that something had to be driving her on this unrelenting campaign to close down the agency that was rendering a needed service to the community. I tried unsuccessfully to get her to let the matter rest so we could begin some bridge building, as I knew that the fallout from the removal of Ms. Penta would be at my door since I was the only one involved with any name recognition.

Ms. Jalpert contacted a reporter with the *Burlington County Times* and provided him with written materials concerning the story, seeking his intervention. By this time, I was convinced that she was not only on a witch hunt with a vengeance but that she was not going to let it go. She was also becoming upset with me because I was not able to see the evil in the agency and endorse her continuing effort to close it down. I realized, much too late, however, that Ms. Jalpert had labeled me as an evil person and targeted me for destruction as well.

In the interim, Emergency Services was relocated to a very nice facility where all of its operations are centralized and updated and is under the direction of very capable leadership. Accompanied by a contract worker from my church, I joined with a group of other volunteers who spent a day, through the United Way of Burlington County, helping to spruce up the new headquarters of Emergency Services. It is ironic that Emergency Services is in a much better position to perform its ministry than it was before the intervention of Ms. Jalpert, but with no thanks to her.

Unfortunately, that was not the end of the story for me and Ms. Jalpert, who later became a volunteer at the day care center of the Alpha Baptist Church. When a staff position became available at the church office she was hired to work full-time. It was during her tenure as the office administrator that I began to see a destructive pattern in Ms. Jalpert's behavior and how she had kept dormant her resentment of me for not continuing the pursuit with her against Emergency Services. She spread false, outrageous rumors about me verbally, and in written form, in an attempt to destroy the Alpha Church and me, the pastor. Many members believed her lies and have left the church. In defense of my name, I have filed a civil suit against Ms. Jalpert, charging her with slander and libel.

What was the real basis for her actions? No one, perhaps, will ever know, but what is evident is the fact that African-Americans are doing more to destroy themselves by their pointless division than anyone from any other race is doing.

Church and Community

The African-American Religious Community

THE ESTABLISHMENT of the first African-American religious community trailed the settlement of the first African-American families by more than a decade. It is almost impossible to fix the exact date when the first house of worship was opened by an African-American pastor. It is accepted without question that the Reverend Davis, pastor and founder of Saints Memorial Community Church, was the first pastor to locate in Willingboro, sometime in the early seventies. However, there was a break in continuity of worship, although there is some uncertainty as to how long the break lasted. He had worship services in different places before actually building the facility where the congregation worships today. By the time that facility was built, Alpha Baptist Church of Christ Nurturing Center had already located in its permanent place of worship.

The first service of the Alpha Church was on June 5, 1977. I was and still am the pastor. It has several distinctions as a minority fellowship. The church was chartered by twelve members: four Burmese, four Koreans, and four African-Americans. The second distinction is that except for the first service of public worship, it has worshiped as a community with its own facility throughout its existence.

The third black pastor in town was the Reverend Ernest Light of the Good Shepherd United Methodist Church. That facility was first built for a white congregation, but when the new St. Paul United Methodist church was built, the white members slowly withdrew from the Good Shepherd church and most of them went to the new St. Paul church. Over the years, there have been a number of smaller African-American religious communities in Willingboro that met in other churches or in homes and schools, a practice that still prevails today.

The fourth African-American church was founded by the Reverend Morris K. Baxter and took the name Cathedral of Love. For many years, that fellowship worshiped in different places, utilizing the Saints Memorial Church for the last few years before moving into its own new structure.

The fifth African-American pastor to lead a congregation was the Reverend Spencer Rogers who took over Delaware Valley Baptist Church when the congregation was rapidly changing from mostly white to almost all black. Today there are a number of African-Americans who are members of churches that have white pastors. As a matter of fact, all of the Willingboro churches pastored by white ministers, with the exception of three, have an African-American membership of 30 percent or more. The exceptions are the Reformed Church, Calvary Baptist Church, and maybe Corpus Christi Roman Catholic Church.

There has never been a very strong bonding among the African-American churches, although they have never been at war either. There is more bonding among some of the white churches because of similarities of rituals of worship. Even that has been limited.

The strongest bond that exists among all the churches is provided through the Willingboro Clergy Association. This group has always been a place where all the participants were equal players, and the lines of communication open and honest.

Dr. Martin Luther King, Jr., Memorial Service

THE ALPHA BAPTIST CHURCH, in January of 1979, initiated the annual memorial service in celebration of Dr. Martin Luther King, Jr.'s, birthday. It soon became the largest and most successful interfaith and cross-cultural event in the history of the township. There are a number of reasons why Alpha introduced the celebratory service. To name a few, Dr. Martin Luther King, Jr., was an American Baptist preacher and attended American Baptist related schools–Moorehouse College in Atlanta, Georgia, and Crozer Seminary in Chester, Pennsylvania. He was a colleague of mine before I became the pastor of Alpha Church, and we had fought together in the Civil Rights struggle in the late fifties and early sixties, although not in the same locations. Above all, Alpha believed it was important to honor someone whose contribution to the struggle for justice had been untiring, unbending, and unending until the day of his death. The Alpha Church thought so highly of Dr. King that they built a memorial park complete with seats, shrubbery, and a marble headstone with his image cut into the stone. It has been maintained and improved over the years and remains the most visible sign, in Willingboro, of his life. When the Alpha Church moved to its new and large edifice at the Alpha Complex, a new and larger memorial was built in honor of Dr. King. The only other recognition awarded to his memory in Willingboro is an elementary school named in his honor.

Alpha sponsored the memorial service alone the first two years.

The response of the African-American community was fantastic. However, the same cannot be said of the white community. For the most part, the presence of the white community was so sparse that they could easily be detected in the audience, and they never remained for the receptions that followed. The services were held in the auditorium of the J.F. Kennedy High School for two reasons. The seating capacity at the Alpha Church (about 75 persons) was thought to be too limited for the expected attendance. This projection proved to be accurate.

The second reason for having it outside of a local church was to provide a neutral site in order to perhaps attract as many people as possible who may not want to attend such a service at a church with a denominational identification and an African-American label. Then there was a third reason. Unfortunately, but historically, many African-American pastors refused to encourage their people to attend a service of this nature unless it was held at their church and sponsored by them.

To help keep the service as a major venue for drawing the diverse community together, the theme was changed each year, more white ministers were placed on the program, and a speaker with name recognition (without regard to race) was invited to give the keynote address. Beginning with the fourth year of the celebration, the pastors from the other two African-American churches in Willingboro were invited to co-host the event with Alpha. The addition of the Reverend Norman Davis of Saints Memorial Community Church and Elder Morris Baxter from the Cathedral of Love Church added a new and much welcome dimension to the service in terms of sponsorship

During the day that the memorial service was held, we added several focused workshops. Each workshop dealt with a different aspect of the racial divide. They were scheduled so that people could attend two workshops if they chose. The workshops ended thirty minutes before the start of the memorial service. Time for a plenary session was built into the workshop agenda. This addition to the memorial service proved to be the most informative and widely attended interracial and cross-cultural event ever held in Willingboro where an opportunity for honest dialogue was provided. During the second sequence of these jointly sponsored services, an unfortunate incident took place. At least it was different, if unfortunate is not the word that best describes what happened. The reader can be the judge.

The pastors of the three sponsoring churches had agreed that one general offering would be taken during a very brief interlude in the program. Each of the pastors had an assignment and Elder Baxter's assignment was to receive the offering. He had no specific instructions from the other two pastors as to how it was to be done. It had also been agreed that all of the expenses for the services would be deducted from the offering first. If there was a shortfall, the deficit would be made up by the participating churches. If there were an overage, the excess would be equally divided in the same manner.

Elder Baxter decided to receive two offerings, one for the speaker and one to help with the expenses incurred by the host churches. This alone was at variance with what we had decided, but to add even a second element in the offering was more than some people could accept, as we learned later. The method he used to receive the offering was as follows: persons willing to give $20 following his lead were to march up to the front first, followed by those who were giving $15, $10, $5, then the rest. This is a method that I have seen practiced in an all African-American congregation but it was totally alien to the white peoples in the audience and to some African-Americans, as well, like the members from Alpha who had never experienced the practice before.

Not only was this procedure time-consuming, but it was also highly embarrassing for many of us, regardless of our ethnic background. Many in the audience (both black and white) left before the service was over. Their early departure could easily be attributed to the way the service had been extended in receiving the two offerings.

We spoke about this matter in the next meeting with the pastors of the hosting churches. Baxter was quite defensive and rightly so, feeling that he was in charge of the offering and had not been given any instructions as to how it was to be taken, which was true, and that the people who were upset were white people and they were not needed anyway, which was untrue. Both Davis and I spoke in disagreement with the method in which the offerings were received due to the nature of the program and that we had thought only one offering would be taken. But as far as we were concerned that was the end of it.

Well, that was not the end of the matter. There was still the meeting of the Willingboro Clergy Association, of which all Willingboro pastors were considered members or potential members. Davis almost never attended any of those meetings and Baxter would only come occasionally. However, both attended this particular meeting. I had been a part of the Willingboro Clergy Association since 1968 because of my position as a denominational executive and as a member of the Parkway Baptist Church.

Before the meeting could get started with the preliminaries, Baxter asked for the floor. He began by saying that he knew some people were upset with the way he had handled the offering, but that did not bother him because white folks were also upset with the way black people worship. There was more to his comments but he closed with the point of view that white people could not pastor black people and that even those who were attending white churches were not getting the best leadership. He then added that even the Willingboro Clergy Association did not really deal with issues facing the black community in Willingboro. There was a sudden outburst of objections to those comments by the white pastors and especially by the Jewish rabbi, who was the senior clergyman in town, but Baxter did not back down. He listened for a while, made a final statement reaffirming his position, left the meeting and has not attended a meeting since. That was about fifteen years ago.

I knew that there was anger on both sides of the racial divide. I could not take the same position of Baxter because it was one in which I did not fully agree and I remained a member of the Willingboro Clergy Association, but I did not want to disassociate myself from Baxter either. I knew that this would be a matter of discussion when the three of us met in our little black group, and I was correct. There was some pressure for me to leave the Willing-boro Clergy Association, but this was softened when I agreed to start a Burlington Council of Black Clergy. I knew that no such animal existed and probably would never amount to much other than a name unless we were willing to put in some real effort to get it off the ground and running. My plate was already full and I did not see how I would have time for additional efforts. But I also knew that the name of the group would carry some weight in the white community, and that weight meant that we would have power as a black church group. I was elected chairman and Baxter was selected as vice-chair. Davis was the person who was going to help pull this coup off.

Well, we let it be known that the group had been formed. We had several meetings among the three of us, but before we reached out to other black pastors Davis died. An associate, who later became Davis' successor attended the meeting and Baxter was made the chairman. The group seemed to have as its main agenda, an

Annual Service in memory of Dr. Martin Luther King, Jr. Because
we now had two separate services, one all black and one integrated,
there was soon a feeling in the community that Baxter and I did not
have much love for each other. This was quietly aired in the black
community, and the whites never knew anything about it. I am sure
that Baxter did the same thing that I did upon hearing such a
comment, which was simply to say that it was not true. We have
most recently had the opportunity to join together in a public
protest against a policy of the School Board and this displayed to
the public what we already knew, that it was our schedules that
kept us apart rather than any personal differences.

When the time came for the next Dr. Martin Luther King, Jr.,
memorial service, Alpha held it alone and it was a huge success.
This was due mostly to the fact that a very energetic young lady had
united with the church and immediately exhibited a burning desire
to become involved in a ministry of the church since she had been
out of the church for ten years. Well, nothing could have pleased me
more, and the responsibility of the annual Dr. Martin Luther King,
Jr., memorial program was turned over to Becky Stevenson (not her
real name), the newest member of Alpha. She took the program and
ran with it. It was expanded to include an essay contest with cash
prizes, which were presented in public along with the winning
speeches. A dinner was added to the format, which followed the
contest. Later Ms. Stevenson added a poster contest for the lower
grades. The response was really tremendous. Even the white
churches, especially the Jewish synagogue, became more visible as
a participating congregation.

Ms. Stevenson recruited persons from other churches to help
with the judging of the essays, which at times reached a number
close to 1,000 entries. She added a catered dinner to the conclusion
of the program for the evening. The ticket sales for the dinner were
so successful that they covered the expenses, and the program
continued to grow bigger and better year after year. At an
unexpected time and from an unexpected source emerged a confrontation that was to have ramifications that extended to a point
that was not clear at the time. The basis of the confrontation can be
attributed to the complaint of a father of one of the contest winners,
which was not handled as appropriately as it should have been, and
the consequences were devastating almost two years after the fact.
What had happened was not really Ms. Stevenson's fault, but she
was in charge of the contest and therefore was responsible for
handling the matter. In summary, this is what happened: The son of

this irate father who did not care for Dr. Martin Luther King, Jr., or the role that he played in the Civil Rights arena submitted the best essay in his grade category and was entitled to the first prize. The father contacted me and asked that his son not be awarded the prize because his son had participated in the essay without his permission. I responded that this was a matter that had to be worked out with the person who was in charge of the contest. However, I gave him a bit of the history of the contest and a little bit of American history as well. He seemed rather satisfied, but still wanted to talk to the person in charge. I gave him the name and telephone number of Becky Stevenson.

I immediately appraised Ms. Stevenson of the telephone call and advised her to talk to the gentleman when he called and that she would have the full backing of her pastor and the Willingboro Clergy Association. Ms. Stevenson did not follow through with the matter, nor did she dispose of it in a professional way. She tended to back off from difficult situations. She ignored the problem and the father was extremely angry. Ms. Stevenson should have surrendered the matter to the Clergy Association since she was unwilling to handle it. This would have allowed the white pastors in town to become involved, since the parent was white. The contest went on, and the son was given his prize in absentia.

We never thought about the issue again until the Alpha Church went before the zoning board to request a variance to enlarge the rear of the house next to the church, which the church owned. It seemed as though the variance was going to be granted until one gentleman on the board stood up and said that he was not going to vote for Alpha to receive the variance and asked all of those who cared about him not to vote for it either. He gave as his reason that he was paying Alpha back for the time when Alpha did not do what he had asked us to do when his son was involved with the Martin Luther King, Jr., project.

Not only did Alpha not receive a variance to add on to the house next door, but the zoning board also took the extraordinary position of withdrawing the original variance from the church. They stated that the original variance had been granted for us to have a limit of 14 people at a worship service, and that Alpha violated that stipulation by having far more than that. Additionally, Alpha was worshiping at hours not permitted when the variance was granted. No amount of explaining by myself or our attorney was sufficient for them to change their minds. In effect, because of the prejudice and anger of one member of the zoning board who had significant influence on the rest of the members, Alpha Church was voted out of existence. However, at that time Alpha promised to take the zoning board members to court for their actions, where we were sure to prevail. A negative racial stand had been taken in a public meeting and this would damage the reputation of the whole town if it were known. A very secret meeting was held between the township manager, the township solicitor, our attorney, and me, and it was suggested by the township representatives that we just sit on that decision by the zoning board and go on with business as usual and the matter would go away. We agreed to this proposal as long as we had the assurance that no actual order would be forthcoming to close down the church, as had been directed by the zoning board. We never had to face the zoning board with that particular issue again, as we elected to build a new church in an area that would be zoned B-1 commercial under the new master plan for the township. This was a compromise that was necessary, if not exactly morally correct.

In the meantime, Ms. Stevenson continued to do an excellent job with the Martin Luther King, Jr. essay and poster contest. We were able to get the Willingboro Education Association involved, and the association designated a person to work with Ms. Stevenson. Ever since that time, the theme of the contest has been developed in cooperation with WEA and Ms. Stevenson's group. The contest has remained successful. In 1997, Ms. Stevenson accepted a call to the Christian ministry and in 1998 enrolled in seminary. She selected someone else from the church to lead the program and remained as a consultant, as she came home from school every weekend. In the meantime, the Willingboro Clergy Association voted to pay for all the prizes that were awarded. There was no contest in 1999 because everyone in the Willingboro school administration office was new except for one or two people. It was felt that we should wait one year until a rapport had been established with the new administration. However, a memorial service was held in January 1999 on a small scale, sponsored by the Willingboro Clergy Association. Since then, we have met with the new superintendent and have been assured of her support for the program and we should be back on track by September 1999, when work on the 2000 program will commence.

We have a young couple from the Alpha Church that have qualified to give leadership to the program and although they are young, we feel certain that they will do an excellent job with everyone working together. To let this program fade away will be abandoning the only program that we have in Willingboro that brings together such a diverse audience and involves so many people. We simply cannot afford to let that happen at a time when all of our efforts should be geared toward rebuilding Willingboro.

Spiritual Leaders in the Prison System

RECRUITING CHAPLAINS of African-American descent has been a problem for the state for well over a half century. It wasn't until the 1980s that the first two full-time African-American chaplains were hired within the prison system. They were Joseph Ravenelle, who rose to the position of chief of chaplains at Trenton State Prison, and William Barrett, who was a chaplain at Rahway State Prison. Both these chaplains were endorsed by the Progressive National Baptist Convention, a predominantly black group with approximately 2.5 million members. Joseph Ravenelle was also endorsed by the American Baptist Churches. At the time, I was responsible for all chaplains within the Progressive National Baptist Convention. I also maintained relationships with the American Baptists.

It was under Barrett's leadership that the first church, the Reconciliation Church of Christ, was organized and incorporated completely behind the prison walls. Developing a constitution and a set of bylaws was a real challenge, since it had never been done before. Gene Reichter, Assistant General Secretary of the New Jersey Council of Churches, and I took on the leadership role for developing the constitution and establishing a judicial relationship of this innovative church with the larger church bodies.

I was recently reminded that when the Reconciliation Church of Christ opened its doors to the inmates of Rahway State Prison for the first time, I had the privilege of preaching the first sermon, entitled, "On a Clear Day You Can See Rahway." It was a moving experience, as a few people who had been former inmates and were converted inside the prison, attended the inaugural service along with other inmates and dignitaries. This was not just a church in concept; it was a fully functioning church, including a choir and policy board.

Ironically, it was this church that proved to be the hindrance to Chaplain Barrett's continued ministry at Rahway. There were some accusations from the administration regarding the use of funds for the church, funds that were not specifically designated for that work. In fact, there was a question as to whether outside funds could be allowed to come into the institution at all. Barrett fought for the constitutional and corporate right of the church to receive funds, and for his right as pastor to provide guidance relating to the use of any funds received. The administration did not relish the idea that Barrett was also the pastor of a congregation in South Bound Brook, New Jersey. As his representative, we could defend his right to pastor the congregation in South Bound Brook as long as the people were aware of his serving as a chaplain at Rahway, as the two were not related in any way. However, we did not get invited to be involved in the other phase of the administration case against Barrett, which ultimately resulted in Barrett being suspended from his civil service position as chaplain. We tried to stay in contact with Barrett, but the wound caused by the disrespect for his work and ministry was very painful, and we lost touch with him at a time when he probably needed us the most. The last we heard, he had taken retirement.

Joseph Ravenelle retired with distinction from his position at Trenton State Prison and continued to serve in ministry by opening a street ministry in Trenton to assist the less fortunate. As of 1998, his ministry was still going strong.

Apart from the two Protestant chaplains, the Nation of Islam had a full-time chaplain as well. They also had a number of assistants working with the chaplain. Since the ordination standards were set by each judicatory, the Islamic group was able to bypass some of the rigid requirements that the Protestants had to adhere to. This also held true for the Jewish and Catholic chaplains, although the chaplains in these latter two instances were highly trained in accordance with their religious endorsing bodies. It should be pointed out that the Jewish presence was very much felt on the Chaplaincy Consulting Committee, although there were very few Jewish inmates behind the walls.

We saw racism in the chaplaincy group raise its ugly head when the director of the chaplaincy left for another position within the United Methodist Church. Many on the selection committee noticed that the field of candidates had prior experience in chaplaincy work, but not within institutions with blacks. At the strong urging of our black chaplains and a few others, I allowed my name to be placed into the mix of candidates for the position to see if a black man would be chosen. (I did not really plan on accepting the position if it were offered.) At that time I was national director of the Home Mission Board of the Progressive National Baptist Convention (the board that had jurisdiction over all chaplains), an endorsed American Baptist, and a member of the Federal Bureau of Chaplains, and I had more units of Clinical Pastoral Education (CPE) than any other person serving as a chaplain or seeking the position of director of chaplains. Although I was better qualified than any other candidate, I was not considered because of my race. A confrontation would have been worthless because I knew that the system was not ready for a black person to preside over all the chaplains in the state–Protestant, Catholic, Jewish, and Moslem. However, the learning experience was well worth the involvement. Then the word came that Commissioner Faubas was going to make the appointment, assuming from our committee the authority that we had fought long and hard for. The new director, a white minister, was appointed through the intervention of the commissioner.

I had become a bit ill from overwork and too little rest. Additionally, I had changed positions by becoming full-time pastor of the Alpha Baptist Church, but agreed to remain on the committee to help the new director, as this would be needed as he dealt with the black chaplains.

Although the African-Americans represented a majority of the inmate population, the vast majority of persons who conducted volunteer religious services within the prisons were white. This may seem like a very lopsided display of compassion, and perhaps it was, but not without cause. Having served as the vice chairman for the Chaplaincy Consulting Committee for more than a decade, I saw plenty of evidence that the prison was not a place for young African-American women who were not properly trained to be involved. More than a few marriages were destroyed, and young girls became pregnant by fast-talking African-American males. In the first instance, it happened while they were still inside and in the latter instance, it reflected a love affair that started behind bars. This was not the case with white women because most of them had men with them, or men led their teams.

It would not be appropriate to leave this brief section of the history of the African-American in the correctional system without mentioning the untiring and unsurpassed work of Mrs. Audrey Kaufman of the Shiloh Baptist Church in Trenton, who for many years performed some outstanding volunteer work. For example, at Christmas time she would prepare special meals for more than a hundred inmates.

Building Alpha Church

THE ALPHA CHURCH continued to grow and eventually ran out of space, and as we ran out of space we knocked out another wall. Over the next several years, there were about seven different renovations and additions that took place in the Alpha Baptist Church. In 1992, Alpha had grown to about 600 members and we could no longer expand, so we purchased land on Rose Street. The church voted to sell the building at 175 Somerset Drive and relocate to the new site and construct a new church. In the process, we changed the name again from Alpha Baptist Nurturing Center to the Alpha Baptist Church of Christ Nurturing Center.

Before any building began, we conducted a feasibility study to confirm the decision to build, what type of facility the members wanted, and how much money they wanted to spend. Next, we designed and implemented a capital funds campaign. I recruited and trained some excellent leaders and workers from among the membership to direct the campaign. More than half the church was involved in some phase of the ten-week campaign. At the victory dinner celebration, we announced that we received approximately $250,000 in pledges. Members also committed to buying selected items for the kitchen, music room, and pastor's office. Other members pledged to purchase crosses for both the interior and exterior. As far as I know, Alpha was the first African-American Church in South Jersey to conduct a capital funds campaign for the purpose of building a new church. I give the credit to the people for their loyal support, but the glory and praise go to God for providing the reason for the new church.

During the campaign, the Willingboro Christian Assembly offered to purchase our original church building for $285,000. After we agreed to sell, but before we signed an agreement with the Willingboro Christian Assembly, we had another offer for $325,000 cash. I know we could have walked away from the lesser offer without any legal redress, but after lengthy discussions we all agreed that we should honor our word and sell the building to the Willingboro Christian Assembly.

With the sale of the building (the property belonged to Cookie and me, but the church paid for some of the later additions, therefore, when it was sold, we requested that we be given a note for a portion of the sale price), we paid off the mortgage on the land. With the remainder and the pledges to give, we had about $388,000–not nearly enough for a project of the magnitude that the building committee planned. We borrowed $455,000 from the American Baptist Extension Corporation, so in total, we had about $843,000. This seemed like a lot of money, sufficient to build a church of superior quality and adequate size. We were wrong. The final cost of the church was approximately $1.25 million, almost $400,000 over budget. The additional costs were due to agreed-upon changes to the plan, like air-conditioning and a carport, as well as unexpected costs for engineering plans, inspections, and county and township fees.

God always knows what we do not, and so we simply rolled up our sleeves and began the initial phase of the project–identifying an architect and builder.

After researching several options, we agreed to hire the Maranatha Company, a Christian company based in South Dakota that specialized in church construction. The Maranatha Company provided all the architectural drawings and the steel framing for a single package price in the range of $162,000. We could hire them to do all the construction, or we could do the rest of it ourselves. If we did the construction ourselves, we could not deviate from any of the specifications submitted to us by the Maranatha Company or our warranty would be void. We opted to do the construction ourselves.

I accepted the responsibility of project manager and oversaw the project from beginning to end. Little did I know that I'd be on-site roughly fourteen hours a day, including most Saturdays and some Sundays after worship. I juggled my pastoral duties, which alone had kept me busy full time. Over the years, I'd developed the practice of making daily visits to members who were in the hospital, offering up to six months of pre-marital counseling for engaged couples, writing my sermons out in full, and never preaching the same message twice. Additionally, there would be deaths that needed to be eulogized, babies to dedicate, candidates to instruct and baptize, individuals and families to be counseled, and church and community meetings to attend.

Cookie was a great support at this time. She spent all her free time with me at the work site helping in many areas–keeping records, providing lunch, running errands, and even helping with construction.

We hired a superintendent and a construction crew, and began work on the foundation for the building. I mention the foundation because of the meticulous details involved in setting all of the anchor bolts in the exact place along the perimeter of the footing for the vertical steel columns to be fastened. Since the Maranatha Company had laid out the structure by computer, and the steel manufacturer had developed each of the hundreds of different segments to those prescribed specifications, there was no room for error. Maranatha told us that if one bolt was off as much as one-sixteenth of an inch, it could throw off the entire structure. If several bolts were off by that much, then the steel structure would be useless. With a fifty-foot span between each major column, it meant that we could not be off center with any of the eight 600-inch spans.

I decided to measure everything twice. After the super-intendent measured the distance and marked where the bolt was to be set in the concrete, I re-measured. He was a little upset by my following him with my measuring tools; he probably thought I didn't trust him. I explained that humans can make errors; it had nothing to do with a lack of trust. He understood, and I kept re-measuring.

When the Maranatha Company arrived to do the steel framing, they re-measured a third time. They said this was the first time they had ever seen a job done so perfectly. Within three weeks, the Maranatha crew completed its work and not one bolt was out of place in any direction.

We estimated that it would take approximately five months to complete the remainder of the building, but due to unforeseen difficulties–such as faulty screws that needed to be replaced and bad weather conditions–it took six. Another difficulty that could have become a disaster became a miracle. About halfway through the project I had to terminate the superintendent because I was not satisfied with his work ethic. When he left, so did his crew. That same day, God provided enough laborers, right off the streets, to continue the work without interruption.

During the actual construction, members from the church worked to help keep costs down, although we did hire an electrician, a heating and air-conditioning specialist, and a plumber. The plumber allowed our volunteers to assist. Our church members also painted, tiled floors, decorated bathrooms, and did anything and everything they were capable of.

The completed building is quite unique. The church is octagon in shape and the interior distance between any of the eight sides measures one-hundred-twenty feet. As we followed the plans in constructing the building, we noticed that there were indeed some features that make it quite different from anything we had ever seen before. In the sanctuary, the ceiling is suspended in such a way that it has a perfect pitch, resulting in a dome-like appearance. In its center is a magnificent skylight. It is the first and only building of its kind and size in Willingboro.

A tremendous disappointment for our hardy members was when the fire inspector, shortly before our dedication service, informed us that all the fire alarm levers had to be moved up four inches before the building could be occupied. We had already planned the dedication, so building inspector Leonard Mason kindly allowed us one hour in our new building, as he stood watch. We thanked God and Mr. Mason for the one hour.

On the day of our dedication service, October 19, we drove in a motorcade from the old Alpha to the new Alpha at 15 Rose Street in Willingboro. It was quite a victory celebration for our rather small congregation. We were moving into a 12,500 square foot building that we had built ourselves in a nontraditional way. Our new home was a magnificent structure to the glory of the Lord.

Dream of a Youth Center Deferred

FOR ALMOST ALL of 1990, Victor Smith and Linda Taylor, both African-Americans and former members of the Willingboro Board of Education, pursued their dream of creating a youth center for Willingboro. Their vision was to transform the former John F. Kennedy High School into a state-of-the-art youth center that would serve the needs of all youth from pre-teen to early adulthood. A detailed proposal was developed that included a comprehensive recreational program that provided opportunities for sports enthusiasts to satisfy their every interest. They did not overlook any aspect in the total development of youth, as many programs geared toward academic, social, and cultural enrichment were included in their proposal. Also included in this dream package was a staffing pattern for each area of the program, along with a detailed budget for the same. The plan called for an initial outlay of funds from the township but once the program was up and running it would become self-supporting.

The two approached me with the idea after they had struggled in vain to gain sufficient support for their proposal. After a couple of sessions with them, where we discussed the idea of the youth center, I decided to talk with the township manager, Sadie Johnson, about the proposal. Mrs. Johnson, who was also a certified public accountant, told me that the budget aspect of the proposal was workable and that it was a good idea. Hearing that response, I suggested that the proposal be placed before the citizens of Willingboro in the form of a referendum and let them speak. She promised to look into my suggestion. When I contacted Mrs. Johnson again, she told me that the council was not in favor of placing it before the citizenry as a referendum and since she worked for council, there was nothing that she could do about it.

Unfortunately, the members of the African-American community who knew about the proposal did not press the members of council, some of whom were African-Americans, for support of a referendum, which resulted in the dream of a youth center being deferred.

As strange as it may seem, I never spoke to a single African-American who did not think that a youth center was a good idea and should have become a reality. The response I heard most often for not getting involved was that those in power were going to do what they wanted to do and their single voice would not make a difference. I knew that they were correct, and the tragedy is that those in power have a way of distracting the public they serve away from those ideas that may even be good for them, even if they do not personally want them. This will always be the case until the public begins to say enough is enough and unite in the struggle for creative change. In this instance, which occurred nearly a decade ago, the dream of the youth center was deferred, but one wonders what other values of youth were deferred along with this dream.

Willingboro's Hall of Fame

I AM NOT AN AVID sports fan and very seldom read the sports page of the newspapers, although I read the papers daily and I have observed that the *Burlington County Times* has perhaps the best coverage of sports in the Burlington County area of any newspaper that is circulated in the county. It is one thing not to be a sports fan but quite another not to recognize the important role that sports plays in any society and with those who make this possible.

There is no way for anyone who has lived in Willingboro for any period of time to let the high achievement of Willingboro athletes go unnoticed. Willingboro's athletes have succeeded in many areas of sports as far back as I can remember. With that thought in mind, it seemed appropriate that there should be some recognition given to those persons who had brought great honor and high visibility to the township because of their superior abilities and talents in sport activities.

One day while playing one-on-one basketball with my grandson, who said that he wanted to be a great star in that game when he grew up, I asked him to name some players in the game. I was pleasantly surprised that he knew quite a few, almost none of whom I knew. It was at that moment that I thought of the idea of having a Hall of Fame to give some much-needed recognition to athletes who had exhibited great athletic prowess in the field of sports. This idea was further enhanced when I attended an event at the Bristol Township High School whereby a member of our church was being recognized by his school for the achievements that he had made in sport activities; in this instance, it was wrestling. I asked myself why that school in Bristol, Pennsylvania, was able to have such a tremendous program of recognition for its athletes, former and present, and Willingboro was not doing the same thing.

Taking the cue from my grandson and adding the experience from the program in Bristol, I concluded that Willingboro should have its own Hall of Fame. I contacted a small number of known sports-minded people and inquired whether they would be interested in coming together to discuss the idea of creating a Hall of Fame for Willingboro. I set a date and invited persons within the Alpha Church, and others who were not members of the Alpha Church, to this initial gathering. Everyone who was invited came and they all thought it was a good idea, and during the discussion it was mentioned that another group had an idea of starting a Hall of Fame as well. I immediately suggested that we try to contact those persons and invite them to our next meeting in order for us to combine our efforts and not be working on the same idea but at cross-purposes.

The other group was headed by the principal of the Penny-packer School in Willingboro, Mr. John Grinnage, so he was invited to attend the next meeting.

During the discussion at that meeting, which was held at my home, where all subsequent meetings were held, it was disclosed that the Grinnage group had indeed been toying with the idea of starting a Willingboro Hall of Fame. However, over a period of time the group had kind of disbanded and the idea of a Hall of Fame had faded into the background.

Mr. Grinnage had maintained great enthusiasm about starting a Hall of Fame and was quite willing to join in with the group that we had started in order to pool our knowledge and resources and make one strong steering committee. In that same meeting it was determined that we would start the Willingboro Sports Hall of Fame. It was our intention that a Hall of Fame for Willingboro would be a positive thing, one that would uplift the community and engender a spirit of cohesiveness amongst the citizens of Willingboro. We also felt that this could help the image of Willingboro, an image that had been eroded by some of the negative publicity that had come from the school board. After much preparation the group determined that we would have nominations for persons to be inducted into the Hall of Fame in chronological order. We would go back historically ten to fifteen years and recognize those persons during that period and then move up to the current period and recognize persons who were making high achievements at the present time.

We received strong encouragement from others who were not on the committee including sportswriters who contributed to the local press, particularly the *Burlington County Times*. Help and encouragement from former athletes, coaches, and sports enthusiasts contributed to the idea of the Willingboro Sports Hall of Fame. We divided the group into several committees with specific functions that would help them move more smoothly with the idea of the inauguration of the first athletes in the Sports Hall of Fame of Willingboro.

It was determined that we would have a large celebration that would be held at the Landmark Inn on Route 38 in Maple Shade on May 21, 1992 to kick off Willingboro's first Hall of Fame. The first class of inductees consisted of William and Evelyn Lewis, the parents of world Olympian Carl Lewis, track; Paul Collins, football, basketball, and baseball; John Gambone, football; Glen Reitinger, football; Dick Luttrell, football; and Bob Vernon, basketball. The day of the actual event turned out to be a very emotional time for the inductees. All of those who were able to attend were extremely proud of having been honored by being selected as the first inductees into the Willingboro Sports Hall of Fame.

After that event was over and all the expenses for it were paid, we had something left in the range of four-hundred-fifty dollars, which we still have in the bank as of this day. We had planned to have another ceremony a few years later for another class of athletes to induct into the Willingboro Sports Hall of Fame. However, this idea faded because we did not get support for our first efforts from amongst either the Willingboro school board or the township council. We did not seek any money from either; we only wanted the school board to give recognition to the efforts that we were putting forth and to perhaps allow a trophy case to be put in the school district administration office, and we only wanted township council to give recognition to the efforts as well, with no monetary request being made. I believe that this is an instance of something that is very good, very promising, and would bring great recognition and benefit to the township, and, at the same time, give proper recognition to those athletes who have made success in their own right.

However, all is not lost; we still have the funds left, many of the same people are still living in the township, and Willingboro is still producing winning teams in different sports. African-Americans must take the lead in any new start-up of the group and solicit the aid and assistance of others because the schools are over 95 percent African-Americans. If it does not happen, the blame will lay at their door.

The Afri-Female Institute

JESSIE GREENE, the vice president of the Willingboro Board of Education, had a vision that one day there would be headquartered in the Willingboro community, a program providing services to African-American females that would be productive, positive, and promising. Joined with three other African-American women, she saw her vision come to fruition when the Afri-Female Institute was incorporated in August of 1998. Currently it is a program that is based in the Willingboro Municipal Complex and operates mainly on Saturday mornings from 8:00 a.m. to 12:00 noon.

The main focus of the programmatic thrust of the Afri-Female Institute is based upon the African tradition, which goes back to the beginning of slavery in this country in 1619 and continued over the following 246 years. The group currently operates on a modest budget and, with volunteer help, is able to render a generous range of services targeting African-American girls in the Burlington, Willingboro, Mt. Holly, and nearby areas, which will enhance their present status. These services will help develop their self-esteem, prepare them for better job opportunities, help them to become better students in school, and generally encourage them to become more productive persons. Given the kind of leadership that is offered through Mrs. Jessie Greene, the executive director, and her co-workers, there is every reason to believe that this group will reach its goals and expand them, just as the Afro-Male Institute has done. (The Afro-Male Institute has headquarters in Burlington and is therefore not a subject for discussion here.)

The only possibility of a threat to the continuing expansion of the Afri-Female Institute will be the non-support by members of the

African-American community. Should that support not be there the prognosis of this group's success will not be positive. On the other hand, if the support is there, then this group will blossom and could become the foremost group within the community that is singularly working for the advancement of African-American females.

Racial Diversity Can Be a Positive Thing

BURLINGTON COUNTY has a huge population, numbering over 400,000 people, by one report, and that includes practically every nationality that's represented in the larger population of the United States. Among the population that has historically been part of the mix is the African-American population. The African-American population is scattered throughout the approximately forty municipalities of the county. However, a large concentration of African-Americans can be found near Burlington City, Mt. Holly, and Willingboro, which would be the hub. In most instances, most eyes focus on Willingboro when there are considerations being made about the stride toward unity among the races. And that is appropriate because Willingboro has moved from a predominantly white community to a community that is now predominantly African-American. The Willingboro community has remained a bedroom community just as Levitt had planned it to be when it was first developed, except his concept was to make it a white bedroom community.

There have not been many significant struggles between the races in Willingboro, except earlier in the integration phase. In fact, throughout Burlington County, there have not been any real efforts toward bringing unity out of the diversity which exists within the four major population groups—white, Latino, Asian, and African-American. It is a sociological fact that diversity need not be a threat to unity and that unity can exist within a diverse population and that existence can create a more productive society for the good of all involved.

It was this thought that led Mary Wells to begin work on the idea of a forum that would have as its main agenda the idea of the effectiveness of diversity. Mary Wells, who is the chief executive officer of Family Service, heads the largest staff that is also more diverse and the most integrated of any of the 23 agencies that responded to the questionnaire I administered that requested these data. Many of the agencies did not give strong evidence of racial inclusiveness on their board of directors, although they serve a diverse population, if not to the extent of Family Service. Other agencies such as Crossroads have a much smaller staff, but the Crossroads CEO is white, even though the majority of the population served is African-American. The CEOs of all the responding agencies were white, except BCCAP's, the county's only anti-poverty program, which has traditionally been led by African-American males. During the past two decades, the position of executive director for BCCAP has been vacant twice and the hiring practice did not change. One of the reasons for this was the fact that BCCAP has been viewed as an agency that serves the needs of African-Americans, which is not the case at all. However, its staff is integrated and the agency serves a very diverse population with a wide range of services.

Mary Wells, however, has a demonstrated commitment to racial justice and stands as a leader among those who struggle for justice among the races. So she was more than happy to host a steering committee that would work on a larger program that would help to bring about racial harmony among the wider community. Several people attended the working sessions on racial diversity, each coming from a different segment of the larger community. Out of that mix grew two concepts; one was the idea of making a video that would show both the negative impact of racial prejudice and stereotypes and the positive impact of racial unity.

The second concept was to have a public forum with leaders from the corporate and community sectors coming together to discuss ways of bringing about more harmony among the races with emphasis upon the African-American community. The forum on racial diversity was hosted by the Alpha Baptist Church in Willingboro, where I am the pastor. I was selected to be the moderator of the forum inasmuch as I had given leadership in that capacity at the earlier meetings that had been held at the facilities of Family Service and hosted by Mary Wells.

We held the forum in connection with the Dr. Martin Luther King, Jr., observance in 1996. There was a significant participation of representatives from the corporate sector, which included Ted Rhoads, vice president of Human Resources at Memorial Hospital in Burlington County in Mt. Holly; Greg Gast, vice president of Human Resources of the Graduate Health System of Rancocas Hospital in Willingboro (the second largest, and it's debatable whether or not it is the largest, employer in Willingboro); Michael DelRossi, vice president of Human Resources of Lockheed Martin in Moorestown; Mary Wells of Family Service, and others in the corporate sector, all of whom were white, as were most of the people in the small audience. Obviously, what was missing was the African-American population, and their absence dealt a deadly blow to the entire project. Whereas, had they responded to this widely-publicized event, there may have been some strides made in the direction of racial inclusiveness which has continued to elude the township and the county.

However, the forum did produce some helpful information, should this idea be tried again and it definitely should. The people present, who represented the corporate sector and nonprofit agencies like Family Service, were people who were committed to racial harmony and justice in the workplace and were already making tremendous strides toward the goal of justice and equity amongst its employees in both hiring and promotion on the job. There has not been a significant effort since then to have another forum, and the idea of the video died out.

I do not want to pitch the blame for the failure to develop the video completely upon the African-American community for a few reasons. One, it was not highly-publicized amongst the African-American community that we were trying to develop a video; and second, the idea of a video was not one that the African-Americans who knew about it could rally support for because of the time frame during which the video had to be made. By the time we were able to find African-Americans who were willing to participate, the project had to be abandoned because the persons who were to make the video could not fit it into the schedule that they were facing at the time. However, given the extent and knowledge of the racial divide that exists in Willingboro in particular and in Burlington County in general, it should not have taken nearly as long as it did to identify African-Americans willing to participate. Thus, once again we lost out as a community because there was not the kind of response that we needed to generate in order to make these projects work.

African-Americans and Economic Development

Minority Economic Development Corporation of Willingboro

THE YEAR WAS 1980, and our town had a well-established African-American population that was growing rapidly, but my wife, Cookie, and I noticed that there was a noticeable absence of any economic development projects owned by African-Americans. We decided that such a venture was necessary to further improve the lives of African-Americans, so we kept our eyes open for some available property suitable for a business.

One day when we were in the hardware store on Charleston Road, the owner told us that the property between his store and the Seven-Eleven was for sale. It was a brick house sitting on little over an acre of land with an asphalt turn-around drive in front.

We decided it would not do any harm to talk to the owner, Mrs. VanSciver, regarding the availability and price of the property. We visited her one Saturday and she welcomed us into her home. She said that indeed she wanted to sell the property for $72,000. Mrs. VanSciver showed us around, and we saw that it had a lot of potential. It was in a commercial area and had a basement with room to expand on the outside. That same day we made the deal to buy the property.

I spoke to a few people in the church and told them about our idea to create an economic development corporation. Cookie and I were interested in talking to anyone who had $500 or more to invest at risk, with the hope of earning dividends on the investment sometime in the future. Well to our amazement, all who were asked and a few who were not asked became investors in the project. A total of about eleven investors put in at-risk capital in amounts ranging from $500 to $10,000. We received $41,000 in investments, and with $10,000 that we had already put down on the property, our mortgage would only be $22,000.

Within a short time, we identified a number of potential tenants. After carefully screening the various businesses, we chose an accounting office, a newspaper, a beauty salon, a small restaurant, and a counseling office.

With all the tenants ready to sign leases, we had to create more parking space as well as renovate and expand the facility. We did all the inside renovations and expansions ourselves. Some days, I worked sixteen hours, most of the time alone, in order to get the place ready for occupancy within our projected time period of two months. We built an addition on the rear, put in a new bathroom, enlarged the kitchen, knocked down walls, built new walls, finished the basement, and divided it into rooms. We also closed up the two-car garage and made it into one large area for the beauty salon. The work on the new kitchen and addition was for the restaurant. The bedrooms were utilized as offices and the basement was for the newspaper office and private storage areas. We secured a loan from the Riverside Savings and Loan Association for funds to construct a parking lot with spaces for twenty-one cars.

All of the businesses in our Minority Economic Development Corporation of Willingboro (MEDCOW) began to thrive almost immediately. The income from the tenants was sufficient to pay our mortgages and other bills.

However, like all new business starts, there were unexpected glitches. The first big one was the restaurant. The restaurant was the project of the Zendars, the Edens, (not their real names) and Cookie and me, all members of Alpha church. The eat-in and take-out restaurant had a built-in problem from its inception–the menu was too large and varied. We served broiled steak, homemade rolls and biscuits, barbecue ribs, homemade pies and cakes, a dozen Oriental dishes, fried chicken, pork chops, pastas, a variety of vegetables, a few house specialties, and a variety of flavors of ice cream, shakes, and banana splits. We simply could not keep up with the orders. People sometimes waited for an hour for their food to be prepared after they had already waited for a seat, in some instances. I knew that we would not be able to remain in business long because we had begun a pattern of deficit spending.

To help us understand our dilemma and improve our operation, I invited a specialist in the restaurant business to come to our place and do an evaluation. He indicated that we were attempting the impossible by having such a wide variety of foods. The second problem was that the space for the restaurant was much too small for an eat-in establishment. He suggested that we do two things: one, trim back the menu and handle specialty dishes only and, perhaps, serve only two meals a day instead of three. The second suggestion, which he was emphatic about, was that we needed to enlarge the facility, even after we made those adjustments. We could accomplish this by knocking out a wall and taking the space for the beauty salon and making it into additional dining room space. The way the business was going, we would make far more from the expanded space than we would with rent from the beauty salon. If need be, another addition could be added for the beauty salon with a side entrance.

When I shared the ideas with the other three partners in the restaurant group, Andrew Eden was vehemently opposed to everything that was suggested. Since I had been handling the breakfast alone and without pay, and another couple had been doing the Asian dishes without pay, we said that the idea was good and that we should go for it. Andrew still balked, saying he could show us how to make money by utilizing the outside and inside without adjusting anything except the menu.

Noticing how angry he was becoming over the issues, we reluctantly yielded to his suggestion—having the world's largest fish fry. We were supposed to make more money from that weekend fish fry than what we made from the restaurant all week.

Although we were not convinced, we were persuaded. Thus we purchased what seemed like a ton of fish. Andrew secured some extra-large skillets and pots for cooking the fish, and we all waited in eager anticipation for the customers to swarm in on Friday and Saturday. Well, the crowd came, but not in large numbers or in a steady flow. In fact, when the weekend was over, we had nearly half the fish left over. (A lot was also lost due to overcooking.)

The whole event was a (fish) flop.

We still had staff to pay and no funds with which to pay them. Cookie and I had used our own funds to help make the payroll. We refused to try the fish fry for a second week in spite of Andrew's plea. Instead, we made the hard but necessary decision to close the doors to the restaurant.

We leased the space that had been used for the restaurant to a lady who wanted to operate a child care center. Acquiring this new tenant prevented us from having to pay for that empty space out of our personal funds.

Just when we thought things had settled down and the facility was fully rented, we faced our biggest challenge of all. I arrived at the facility early, as was my custom, and found that the place looked a bit ransacked, especially the office that was used by the tax and accounting service. Then I found a note on my desk from the public accountant, Lester Yates (not his real name). He asked me to take care of his wife and said that he was sorry about what had happened.

I contacted his wife, but she had not heard anything from him.

Later that evening, the pastor of Tabernacle Baptist Church in Burlington called and informed me that, over a period of nearly a year, the accountant stole upwards of $35,000 from the church's building fund.

When we heard from Lester a day later, he was in Texas. We persuaded him to return to New Jersey, assuring him that we would do all that we could to help in the situation. Lester returned, and the Tabernacle Baptist Church arranged a repayment plan for him. They also required him to take out a life insurance policy payable to the church to be kept in force until the total amount of the stolen funds was repaid.

Lester was the treasurer of MEDCOW, and two people on the Board of Directors insisted that he be removed from office. Lester made a public apology for what he had done and gave evidence that MEDCOW's books were in order. Thus, I supported Lester as a repentant sinner who deserved to be treated as any other person who had done wrong and repented.

But the two board members maintained that he was not fit to come into the presence of the members of the board or have anything to do with MEDCOW. They started a rumble on the board that never did subside.

Next came a squabble in the beauty salon between the two owners. Both were Christians and members of Alpha Church. All of my efforts to try to get them to work together failed, and they both left, going in different directions.

With that space empty, Andrew Eden persuaded me to go into business with him. First he suggested an ice cream parlor, but that didn't pan out. Then he suggested we open a barbershop. He said that he had learned to barber years ago and that his uncle had some used equipment that we could buy cheap. Although I did not know anything about cutting hair, and this was not one of my interests, I agreed. We were to divide the profits appropriately, with him getting 75 percent because he would be servicing one of the chairs, and me getting 25 percent because I would be doing the cleanup and all necessary upkeep of the facility. This seemed fair to me since it would still be fulfilling the dream of economic empowerment for blacks. When the equipment came and the barbershop opened, I went for a haircut. Not only could my partner not cut hair, but he broke our agreement. He told me that his uncle would not sell the equipment to both of us and that my partner would have to buy it alone–he said, therefore, that I could have no part in the business.

To make a long story short, the board, against my better judgment

(I believe the project could have worked given more time), filed for bankruptcy.

The bankruptcy judge appointed a trustee who proceeded to ask for a list of creditors, both secured and unsecured. The property was sold for $120,000. A portion of the $120,000 went to the trustee, and with the remainder we paid off the secured creditors and the unsecured creditors. After the court costs and attorney fees were paid, we were only able to return to the investors 50 percent of their investments. It was a sad ending to what could have been a truly successful story if African-Americans had just learned how to work together.

Federal Housing and Urban Development Fraud

JOHN TEGLEY WAS the township manager when the scandal of corruption in federally-insured housing spread from Camden to Willingboro in 1985. I heard Tegley, make in an informal conversation, the same comment that he made to the press when the rumors first hit the surface: "There have been those sorts of free-floating allegations of unqualified buyers buying homes in this community for years."

John Tegley said that Willingboro's officials had urged the federal government to investigate the patterns in the past but had received no significant response from his request. This was the first time an agency had been able to look at the question of the economics Tegley indicated. He further stated that he believed that they were looking for a pattern of fraud. What the township officials had already discovered by the time the federal agencies got involved was that anybody could have exploited the system. They began to realize that the enemy was not just one person or one agency it was the federal, state, and local systems all playing a part.

The allegations originally centered in Camden when the investigation of housing sales and foreclosures began in 1984 in that town. However, no one in any official capacity within the township of Willingboro was surprised when FBI agents investigating possible fraud in the issuance of federally-insured mortgages subpoenaed sales records from five Willingboro real estate offices. The FBI, the Veterans Administration, and HUD's Office of the Inspector General broadened their probe into the mortgage fraud to examine all those loans made in South Jersey through HUD's Camden service office. The investigation became public after Stephen Springer, a vice president of a major mortgage company, Margaretten & Company, told a federal judge that he had paid more than $20,000 in kickbacks to Howard Ryan, one of Burlington County's most prominent real estate agents, who had offices in Willingboro. When a review of deeds, mortgages, and tax records filed in the Burlington County courthouse was conducted, it showed that Springer and Ryan held joint ownership of fifteen Willingboro houses valued at $685,000.

Springer and Ryan were among those snared in an investigation that led to the conviction of forty real estate brokers, agents, and mortgage company executives in South Jersey. Springer pleaded guilty to making kickbacks and defrauding the government on loans issued by the United States Department of Housing and Urban Development (HUD).

In addition to being charged with receiving $27,000 in kickbacks, Ryan was charged with falsifying employment and credit information for buyers of HUD owned homes, which allowed buyers to obtain loans even though they were not creditworthy.

Records dated from 1980 were also pulled from Calhoun Realty, Candid Realty, March Realty Associates, and Town and Country Realty, all of Willingboro.

Falsified information, including fake employment histories and earnings, bogus social security numbers, and fictitious credit references, enabled unqualified buyers to obtain home mortgages for which they would not normally qualify. In some instances, women on welfare were able to purchase expensive homes. In many cases, because payments were months behind, the government was forced to begin foreclosure proceedings within a year after the sale had been made. Between the years 1980 and 1985, foreclosure proceedings had been completed on about 280 houses.

One pattern of foreclosure in Willingboro stood out as unique. One couple was able to purchase four Willingboro houses in eight years. All of these purchases were financed with government-backed mortgages even though three mortgages were foreclosed on because the couple did not make the monthly payments. Under normal circumstances, the foreclosures would have disqualified the couple from obtaining new federally-backed mortgages.

Three former business associates of Willingboro realtor James C. Calhoun pleaded guilty in federal court to charges stemming from the federal investigation. Calhoun died before any formal sentencing could be made against him.

Insurance agent Charles M. Scott admitted filing a form saying that a nonexistent person drew a salary of four hundred twenty-five dollars a week in his office. He faced a year in prison and a one thousand dollar fine, according to published reports. What we later read was that he did not have to serve any actual jail time but that he did lose his license for a period of time and then subsequently reopened his business.

Charles E. Young, a reported certified public accountant, said he was paid fifty dollars for filling out a false W-2 and 1040A form for a home buyer. The false forms enabled a buyer to receive a government-insured mortgage for a $56,500 home in Haddon Township, Camden County; the mortgage subsequently went into default. At the sentencing the judge indicated to Young that he had to serve some time in jail because he was a public accountant who was being disloyal to his license. Young served his time but I do not know if he is still in the Willingboro area.

Richard Austin, who did contract repair work for Calhoun, admitted he acted as a straw buyer for one home and received mortgages on others while making only minimum payments.

Government agencies that approved applications for federally backed mortgages were painted financial pictures of buyers who were likely able to make monthly mortgage payments. However, in fact, many of the buyers weren't qualified and ended up in foreclosure, sometimes after only a few months. In the end, the mortgage company earned points in origination fees; the real estate salespeople earned commissions, and taxpayers ended up making good on mortgages that failed, which meant that all taxpaying Americans had to contribute to this horrible fraud activity that took place in Burlington and Camden counties—a sad commentary to the history of Willingboro.

Two of the persons who were indicted as a result of this federal probe were African-Americans.

However, one other African-American, who worked for Ryan Realty, did not get indicted and ended up operating his own private realty company. At one point, he had the only realty agency in Willingboro. Today, he has the most visible realty office in Willingboro, although there is at least one other African-American operated agency in the township. However, there are numerous real estate agencies that sell homes in Willingboro that have a diverse staff.

The Alpha Complex

ONE OF LOU RAWLS' most popular hits, "Some Folks Will Never Learn," perhaps applies to me more than I care to admit. After the embarrassing failure of MEDCOW, which did not have to be, I promised Cookie I would never again get involved in a for-profit

venture with black people. While we were building the Alpha
Church in the early 1990s, I violated that promise. I convinced
Cookie that we should give the concept of working toward a joint
venture with our own people one more chance, and this time we
would do it smarter.

Cookie and I, joined by Mamie Waller, contracted to purchase
the balance of the land to the south of the church property. Mamie
Waller, a cosmetologist by trade, operated a beauty salon in
Burlington, New Jersey, and was interested in establishing her own
shop. I was interested in almost anything that the church could
eventually benefit from, and this project would, when it was solvent,
return the money we advanced.

With the approval of the Alpha trustees, we purchased the
property in the name of the church. This was done so the church
would have an immediate share in the land and a future share in
whatever was developed on the land. The church was not in a
financial position to put any funds into the purchase of the land and
would not share in the cost of the amortization of the mortgage or the
cost of the building of any structures on the property. This was
similar to the way the first facility that housed the Alpha
congregation was created. My wife and I had advanced all of the
funds to purchase the building at 175 Somerset Drive and later turned
it over to the church with the idea of recouping most of the money we
had advanced over the years when the property was sold.

About that time, another black woman contacted me because
she and her business partner were interested in building Willingboro's first African-American funeral home. I took her around to
look at all of the places known to me where a building could be
converted into a funeral home or where one could be built. There
wasn't anything that she found acceptable. I told her about the piece
of property in the northwest section adjacent to the church's land.
The church did not yet own this particular piece of land, but Cookie
and I held an option to purchase it at an agreed price, which was far
below market value. The partners liked the site and felt that its
proximity to the church bode well for their venture.

Cookie and I were a bit reluctant to release our option to them
because we were just getting ready to close on the property ourselves,
and we did not know these people very well. We agreed to release the
land to them when they accepted the covenant restriction that we
wanted placed in the deed that specified that whatever was built on
the land must be in harmony with the teachings and practices of the
Alpha Church. A funeral home met that restriction.

Since the funeral home was going to be built next to the church, it was determined that it would be best for the beauty shop to be built in the center of the property adjacent to the proposed funeral home in order to leave the larger portion of land undeveloped. In order to accomplish this, a series of complex cross easements had to be granted between all parties and a subdivision developed. This resulted in the creation of the "The Alpha Complex," which included the entire site.

This seemed a most appropriate name since all establishments present and future depended upon the use of the Alpha parking lot. Construction on Mamie Waller's beauty salon and on the funeral home began at the same time. Although a legal dispute between the funeral home partners has prevented the funeral home, which is currently 95 percent complete, from becoming operational, a recently rendered ruling should bring closure to the matter, if the parties are willing to follow the judge's order.

Mamie's Hair Expo has been completed and is by far the most elegant freestanding beauty salon in the township, a real showplace both inside and outside. She continues to do well, the one happy ending in this business deal so far.

Concurrent with construction of the funeral home and Mamie's Hair Expo, I was still trying to determine what to do with the rest of the undeveloped land. In the meantime, a former church member, Wanda Prescott (not her real name), asked me to assist her with the establishment of a group home for the developmentally disabled under the name of the Alpha Church.. I knew nothing about group homes but agreed to go with her to a couple of seminars in different parts of the state where presentations were made.

After attending two seminars and reading some material on the concept, I saw this as something that the church might be willing to lend its support to, especially since it was going to be managed by a minority woman, and the church would benefit financially as well. Cookie and I, especially Cookie, put in a lot of hours helping with the proposal, which did not win in a highly competitive process.

I told Wanda that we had given all of the time and energy that we had in the unsuccessful effort and now planned to look into developing a day care center on the vacant land across from the Alpha Church. Wanda represented herself as a person who was also interested in day care programs, and mentioned that she was a certified head teacher. This perked up my interest considering the fact that I had always had an interest in a day care center for the church.

Bob Carter (not his real name), a member of the Alpha Church, said that he knew a construction company in Pennsylvania that could erect a building for us at a very inexpensive price. Bob, a graphic artist of sorts, drew up a computer design of what a day care building would look like on the vacant land; Wanda provided the tuition per child being charged by day care providers; and Cookie figured out the student-teacher ratio according to age group.

With this information, I developed some projections regarding the income and expense of operating a day care over a five-year period at varying degrees of capacity. It did not appear that this could be anything but a successful venture.

What convinced me to go along with the idea was twofold. First, it would benefit working parents immediately and eventually provide employment for unemployed or under-employed workers. Secondly, Wanda would be the certified head teacher; Bonnie Carter, wife of Bob Carter, the business manager; our daughter Karen Bass, the office worker; and Cookie, the director.

This was very important because we had limited capital for building and none for start-up operations. Wanda and Bob could make available $10,000 each, but that was hardly enough when we were talking about a building estimated to cost $550,000. We could borrow $150,000, and it seemed that Cookie and I, who were the only ones who had already advanced funds in the acquisition of the land and payments of the mortgage, would have to be putting up a lion's share of the funds. This did not matter as long as we would get them returned in the long term.

The company that Bob recommended presented a proposal that was far too high for us to consider, and we did not even like their depiction of the project. So we decided to go ahead on faith with the project, with me serving as the project manager and lead carpenter.

While the building was under construction, Wanda convinced us that she should be allowed to begin a before-and-after school program in order for us to have some children ready to enter the day care center when our building was completed. She wrote a proposal, which was presented to and accepted by the trustees. The program was to be operated out of the church's fellowship hall, and the church would be paid $300 per week for the use of the space.

Wanda ran the program until the day care was operational but kept postponing the submission of an accounting for the operation and also was failing to make payments to the church as promised. However, the biggest blow of all came when we discovered that Wanda was not certified to be a head teacher, and Bonnie Carter (not her real name) had been paying herself a regular salary. I called for a board meeting and asked for a full accounting of all the operations. There was none available for the before-and-after school program, but we owed the church about $9,000, and the day care was in a deficit operating mode.

To make matters worse, Wanda was asking for a return of her investment funds. I stated that if the $10,000 that she and Bob had each put up was to be called an investment, then we would have to declare the building a for-profit venture. If this were done, we would have to sell the building, by permission of the bank, which held a secured loan on it, and pay the church and all of our other obligations, including a salary for Cookie, who had never received a penny of the salary promised her.

The other alternative would be to consider all the money advanced as loans as subject to repayment and try to bring the day care into an operational mode of financial solvency. This meant that the church would have to accept responsibility for the building, and this required approval.

In the meantime, we had to meet the legal requirement that a certified head teacher spend at least six hours on-site each day. To accomplish that, Cookie had to come to the center for two hours before she went to her teaching job, spend her lunch hour at the center, and return for three hours after school. In addition to that, she stayed for another two hours each day cleaning up the place and preparing it for the next day since she was serving as both director and head teacher. This became too much, and in order to save her health she had to retire from the school district two years prior to the time she had planned.

Cookie and I started the repayment of the money advanced by Wanda Prescott at the rate of $500 per month. She had a lawyer write us demanding $5,000. We agreed to a complete payoff by March 1, 1999, through our attorney. We never heard from her regarding this counteroffer.

During this time but before the financial dispute began, Wanda Prescott had come to me with a problem she was having at her job at Family Service of Burlington County. She and another African-American woman said a white person, with much less seniority than they had and whose experience was inferior to theirs, was hired to a much higher position over them. On the surface, this did not seem just and I promised them that I would speak to the agency's Chief Executive Officer, Mary Wells, concerning the issue and get back to them.

It turned out that the position specifically required that the applicant have a master's degree in social work and neither of them did, but the person who was hired for the position did. This made the matter of experience a moot issue.

Ms. Wells agreed to do whatever was possible to help relieve some of the emotional stress that the two black employees, especially Wanda Prescott, were having. But in anger, Wanda resigned from the agency, enlisted the help of the NAACP, and reported the case to the Division of Civil Rights.

When the case came up before the Office of Civil Rights, I was asked to testify and my testimony was the deciding factor in the case, which essentially concluded that Wanda had not been discriminated against and therefore had no entitlement whatsoever. Wanda became furious with me over the way the case was settled. I knew at the moment that I gave my testimony that I had made an enemy of Wanda, but I am a worker for justice and sometimes justice comes at the expense of peace between two or more individuals.

False accusations and lies spread like wildfire in churches. At about this same time, a music leader in the church accused me of placing seven or eight mortgages upon the church, mortgages that were to benefit me personally. He demanded a forensic audit of the records, which would give evidence that I had stolen perhaps as much as a million dollars from the church.

This was a very serious charge, and he knew that it was not true, but it created sufficient tension in the congregation, and I knew that it had to be addressed. I asked Mamie Waller to convene a special group to conduct an investigation of these charges. She could have on the committee anyone that she chose, and I made a few suggestions for consideration. It was made clear that I would not be on the special task force, and would not be privy to any of its investigations until they made a report to the church. She was told that she could use legal counsel, official title researches, and whatever means the task force desired to accomplish their mission, which was to bring an unqualified report of every transaction that had been made in the name of the church, the day care, and the beauty shop. They had the privilege of holding their meetings any place they desired and could take as long as needed to produce a definite report.

Miss Mamie's task force conducted their investigation with meticulous detail. All of the records were searched, legal counsel consulted, and a conclusion was reached. The special task force concluded that I had not placed any mortgages upon the church, illegally or otherwise. In fact, there was only one mortgage on the church and that was from the loan acquired when the church was being built.

The task force revealed that the church owed me $174,000, which represented money loaned to the church during the building phase of the new facility. It also included the $40,000 that my wife and I deposited on the land where the church was built. Finally, it was shown that without the personal sacrifice of funds from my wife and me, the church would never have been built. (Cookie and I had purchased the building in which our old church was located two years before Alpha was organized. When that property was sold for $285,000 the funds were turned over to the Alpha Church, which never had purchased the building in the first place. This is a matter that still must be cleared.)

This saga continues to haunt me today. Currently, for reasons beyond my knowledge, the attorney general of the state of New Jersey has subpoenaed all of our records from the church; the Alpha Community Outreach Program, which operates the Alpha Child Care and Developmental Center; and Mamie's Hair Expo. Both the church and Mamie have hired attorneys. We know that someone is accusing us, primarily me, of wrongdoing of a criminal nature, as that would be the only reason the attorney general would be seizing our records. This much is certain: whoever our enemies are, they have made some convincing allegations to the attorney general about our alleged criminal activities. And depending upon the result of the investigation, the charges could be turned over to a grand jury that could hand down an indictment based solely on flawed information. If so, I will have to defend myself, although I know that I have done nothing criminal in my whole life. Since this is, perhaps, the court of last resort for my enemies, I expect all the stops to be pulled, and every conceivable lie that can be conjured up to be told under oath, by people that I might never have thought would turn against me. If the allegations of Wanda Prescott and Bob Carter are any indication, then the worse is yet to come.

Despite all that, I am determined that we, as a minority people, will be able to leave something behind us that other people can see and emulate. The Alpha Complex is a project that will not fail, its success is already in place and accounted for and we can be very proud of that.

NAACP and Alpha Day Care in Dispute

WEDNESDAY, JULY 9, 1997, I picked up the *Burlington County Times* and read the headline: "NAACP-church in dispute over day care." I was shocked to read what followed.

> Allegations have been raised against a church and its day-care center by the president of a local NAACP branch. Accusations of violating ethical standards were made against the Reverend Joseph Bass, Pastor of Alpha Baptist Church on Rose Lane. They were issued yesterday by Roosevelt Nesmith, president of the Cinnaminson-based South Burlington Branch of the NAACP. The dispute between the two prominent local African-American figures concerns a woman who had been working as a day-care teacher for the church.
>
> Ethel Jackson (the woman in question) says her trouble with Reverend Bass began after a physical confrontation involving her and another congregate following services on Palm Sunday this year ...According to Jackson and Nesmith, she was fired. But Rev. Bass said she simply stopped showing up for work. Jackson subsequently filed a complaint with the NAACP, prompting an investigation by the branch, Nesmith said. Nesmith claims Jackson and other day-care employees are overworked and underpaid by day-care management, and that classrooms are overcrowded. He is calling for a managerial housecleaning at the center. "We have put this on our front burner, and want to let the people know how bad it is at this daycare center," Nesmith said, alleging children are the ultimate losers in this feud. Rev. Bass agreed children would be harmed by the dispute. Rev. Bass denied Nesmith's allegations, and argued Nesmith is only trying to smear his name due to lingering animosity over earlier litigation in which Bass was a witness against Nesmith.
>
> "He vowed to destroy me, and he has tried in every way to do that," Reverend Bass said. Nesmith said Revered Bass has not been as cooperative with the NAACP's investigation. "Their attitude to us was shocking." he said, "and I never witnessed anything like this in my life."

This article sent smoke up all over the county and sparked a fire that will not die down for years to come. I felt so angry and betrayed over the actions of that newspaper reporter. I had spoken to the reporter late the previous night, and I told him the allegations were not true and that he should check with the Division of Youth and Family Services the next day. But he did not wait to verify the facts.

The *Trenton Times* ran a more accurate version of the story, after checking the facts with the Division of Youth and Family Services the next day. July 10, 1997, The Times carried the following story:

> State officials have found no basis for allegations made by the county chapter of the NAACP of abuse and improper supervision of children at a local church-run child-care center.
>
> The allegation grew out of efforts by the local NAACP chapter president to mediate an employment dispute between the pastor of the church and a former member of the congregation who had worked for the child-care center.
>
> Roosevelt Nesmith, president of the South Burlington Chapter of the National Association for the Advancement of Colored People, said he asked the state Division of Youth and Family Services to investigate the welfare of children at the Alpha Child Care and Developmental Center after what he described as a "hostile" meeting with the Rev. Joseph O. Bass and center supervisor Peggy Johns to discuss the employment matter. Nesmith said after the June 16 meeting with Bass and Johns, he felt he "definitely had reason to fear for the children," solely because of Bass' and Johns' manner.
>
> "These people never should be supervising young kids with their attitude, Nesmith said. "Can you imagine the attitude they have to the children?"
>
> On Tuesday, Newsmith also issued a news release accusing Bass of "unethical and unprofessional treatment, employee rights violations, illegal labor practices."
>
> DYFS, which must respond to all allegations of abuse, conducted a surprise inspection of the center on Monday and found nothing to support Nesmith concerns.
>
> Wendy Patella, spokeswoman at the Department of Human Services that runs DYFS, said the bureau that licenses child-care centers inspected the child-care center Monday. "We didn't substantiate any of the allegations of abuse or improper supervision," Patella said.
>
> Sandy Feldman of the Bureau of Licensing said an inspector interviewed numerous children and examined the child-care center and could find nothing amiss. "'We saw no indications of poor supervision whatsoever," Feldman said.
>
> Everything is 100 percent in order," Bass said. "Each and every charge is unfounded. We have a spotless record." Nesmith toured the child-care center. "The NAACP is jumping the gun, Bass said. "The NAACP is doing a grave wrong not only to us, but to the NAACP."

I didn't think that would end the mess, and just as I predicted it did not. The next day after the release of the report by DYFS clearing us of all charges, Nesmith contacted them again with a complaint and new charges. The complaint was that the inspectors who made the surprise inspections of the Alpha Child Care Center were inexperienced and did not know what they were doing or what to look for. He demanded a second secret inspection by more advanced staff. DYFS, knowing they were dealing with a powerful organization in the NAACP, agreed and made two additional surprise visits with more senior staff The results were the same: they found nothing out of order, and the charges were again baseless.

So much damage was done in such haste, and there was little to be done about it after the fact. I did, however, talk to the editor of the paper and wrote the following letter to the editor, which the *Burlington County Times* printed in its entirety:

> Although a certain event of July 9 is now history, it will still be remembered by many citizens of Burlington County's African-American community as one of the darkest days in the long saga of Willingboro. On that fateful day, the *Burlington County Times* carried, as its lead story, "NAACP-church in dispute over day care." There are a number of reasons why this story had such negative impact:
>
> 1. It was over-exposed. Of all the people in the journalism profession with whom I spoke-those who had seen the story and those who reviewed my fax (it had been faxed to journalists out of the state for evaluation) —no one thought it should have made the front page of a quality newspaper.
>
>   It was not like the bombing of the World Trade Center or a Federal Building. It was not a plane-hijacking with fatalities. It was not a serial killer on the loose, nor was it even a train wreck with no deaths. It was a simple list of allegations against one day-care facility made by Roosevelt Nesmith of the South Jersey Branch of the NAACP, whose motives should have been questionable based upon the content of the story itself. It was definitely not worthy of the front page.
>
> 2. The story was poorly reported and the information badly handled. A vital factor in the story was presented in reverse form, and would have provided the reader with a clearer view of the nature of the story had it been correctly reported. The BCT made a clarifying statement the next day on the second page, which was OK, but the explanation was too late. Who

read it and connected it with the original headline release?

Additionally, the *BCT* reporter should have checked his sources more carefully, especially since it was destined for the front page. I had personally indicated what the facts were and where he could obtain verification of the same. This was based on the results of two surprise visits by inspectors from the state Division of Youth and Family Services, who had been to our day-care center earlier in the day and cleared us of all the NAACP's allegations. I suggested that the reporter check my comments against the DYFS report. He could not wait, because the story was too hot to sit on for another 24 hours.

Within an hour after I talked to the *BCT* reporter, a *Trenton Times* reporter called. I gave the same response to that reporter with the request that he check it out and therefore avoid printing a misleading story that could potentially harm the children, the center and Alpha Baptist Church. The *Times* reporter had the good judgment to recognize that he was dealing with a potentially damaging issue that could do an immeasurable disservice, so he investigated and later reported the story factually. Such excellent reporting is rare, but needed.

Since then, and even as I am writing this letter, my phone is ringing with people calling about the *BCT* story. The calls, questions and comments have been the same: Why did the *BCT* make it a front-page story? Why did they not wait to check facts? When they were supplied with the facts, why wasn't that given the same prominent space on the front page that the first story was given?

3. However, the preponderance of their comments tended to suggest that the *BCT* is more interested in dividing Willing-boro than it is in trying to help heal the racial divide. It does little good to suggest that this was not a matter of race. Indeed it was, and the *BCT* helped make it so.

And yet, because of my long and wonderful experience with Marvin Ellis, the *BO*'s late publisher who truly believed in justice and fairness for all; my limited but positive experience with present publisher, Stan Ellis, whom I hold in high regard; and also executive editor Ronald Martin, I cannot allow myself to believe that what is so apparent is equally real. I want to believe that the *BCT* is not a racist paper and that they do not take any pride in this debacle.

In any event, we at the Alpha Center, leaders in the drive for racial harmony in our community, county and state, must work harder because of stories such as these. If the *BCT* is truly in this fight to help make racial and cultural diversity work, there will be other opportunities to demonstrate the same. Together we can make a difference.

Until the next test comes, we can be hopeful, can't we?"

Since that day, July 17, 1997, the *BCT* has been reporting more good news regarding African-Americans, especially in connection with Black History Month in February 1998 and in February 1999. They have also hired their first full-time African-American, who was in the first few months of his employment when this story was released.

Willingboro Defeats Liquor Sales Referendum

FOR THE THIRD TIME, Willingboro voters turned down a binding referendum put forth by council that would have permitted on-site liquor licenses to be purchased by the Willingboro Country Club and establishments along Route 130. The proposal would have restricted alcohol to be sold by the glass and only in those establishments with a seating capacity of at least 150 people with no more than 30 patrons being allowed to sit at the bars. However, it still was unacceptable to the Willingboro Clergy Association, which waged a campaign against it.

Since I was president of the clergy association at the time, it often fell upon me to give the position of the clergy on the issue. Our position was quite simple—we did not agree that five restaurants would be the economic salvation of the vacated Willingboro Plaza, nor should it be. We felt that alternative means should be sought to revitalize the plaza. Equally important was the fact that most of us were part of denominations that opposed the sale and use of alcohol as a beverage.

It was a hard-fought campaign, especially on the part of the council because they had the dollars. They bought television advertisements and other media ads, and we did not have funds for either. My church produced flyers opposing the referendum and distributed them within the community, and all of us spoke about the issue from our church bases.

In the end, the vote, although close, was against the referendum. That was in 1997, and the judge said that it could not come up again until 2003. This is an indication of what can happen when people work together on an issue of importance even when they are up against opposition with more power than they have.

School and Government

School Controversies in Willingboro

CONTROVERSY, POLITICAL POSTURING, board infighting, name-calling, members walking out of the meetings, disrespect among the members, and many other negative patterns of behavior cast a negative shadow upon the Willingboro Board of Education meetings and the entire public school district. Much time is wasted on non-productive issues that could be utilized to perform the tasks for which the board members were elected to do, and that was to set policies and monitor the administration of those policies rather than attempt to micromanage the district, which is the task of the superintendent they hired.

I cite an example to make the point. One member on the school board participated in a discussion before the board that involved the church where he was an officer. The issue concerned the request that would allow his church to rent property from the school board. This board member should have abstained from participating in a discussion of the matter because it was clearly a conflict of interest. That situation led to the attorney for the school board to resign the position of board attorney and another member of the school board to file a complaint with the State Ethics Relations Commission charging that this member violated the law by participating in negotiations in which he had a personal interest because he was a deacon of the church that was asking for a consideration from the board.

Over the years, the actions, and failures to act, by members of the board have been such that the reputation of the district has deteriorated to a level that one member referred to recently as the worst in the history of the district. Today that long pattern of fighting, arguing, and micromanaging the district has now become a part of the pattern of the district and is viewed by many on the outside as one of the most negative features of the entire district. Therefore, it is of no surprise, even to the casual observer, that any suggestion that comes before the school board is going to be the basis of a new round of arguments, whether it is a good suggestion or a poor one. Neither is it a surprise to any observer that any member of the school board may, at any given time, take a stand that may seem right to that board member but is not acceptable to other members of the board or to the next level of authority over the board. Or a board member may participate in a discussion of an issue before the board where there is a conflict of interest.

The board vote, which favored the church, created mixed emotions within the community. Some felt that the church, as a faith community, had taken a bold stand by seeking to provide an opportunity for children to receive an education outside of the district that would provide core values resulting in the best possible student. And they felt that because of this alternative form of education, the church should not only be complimented but should also be given special considerations when it came to the rental pricing structure.

Others in the community felt that the laws separating church and state were very clear and the church, although having the right to operate its own school, should not be given any special considerations in the rental rates at the taxpayers' expense that would place it in a more favorable position than the other tenants.

Two elements contributed to the controversy. One, the board did not follow the advice of their counsel, which provoked the counsel to resign, and two, the board did not ask the board member who was also a member of the affected church seeking the contract to excuse himself and stay out of both the discussion and the vote.

The Ethics Commission ruled that the member from the church was being pulled in two different directions at the same time, one loyal to his church and the other loyal to his school board responsibilities. Since he did not voluntarily recluse himself from the discussion, he placed himself in a position where it was clear that this action on his part warranted a recommendation for censure. However, the board did not read the letter of censure until after midnight, when the members of the public had virtually gone home. Therefore, reading of censure was not effective, thus contrary to its intent. Because the censure was read at a time when it could not have its intended impact it was required to be read a second time. The fact that it had to be read a second time created real tension on the board and stress for the individual from the church. The fact that it was read the first time at such a late hour suggested to some members of the community that this member had more influence on the board than he should, especially in an area where he should have recused himself. On the other hand, there are those who told me that it was good that he was on the board to influence the decision in favor of his church; otherwise, his church might never have been able to obtain the facilities and thus not be able to expand their school.

It is these kinds of actions that have generated mixed patterns of thoughts among members of the Willingboro community toward the board of education. People continue to believe that whoever has the strongest political position on the board and can sway five of its members will be the determiner of how a vote will go on any given issue and may not have any relationship to the merit of the issue at all. Therefore, one never knows how a decision is going to go down except that it is going to go the way any five members want it to be. In many instances this is not always clear or positive, as in the instance involving the church.

The same thing is true when the decision was made by the board to decline the request of the Family Alliance Charter School to rent space at the school where the church also runs a school. Was there a good and sufficient reason for the Willingboro Board of Education to disallow the charter school to rent space in the Stuart School where it also rents space to the church and still has space available? The charter school is a public school, but privately managed. The rental structure that was offered by the charter school was greater than that offered by the church. Would renting space to the charter school place it in direct competition with the school that is run by the church? If so, would that have been a bad thing or a good thing? It is not for me to answer that question; however, are charter schools to be an alternative to the regular public school and also a challenge to them? Should it be different for a private school? By state law, charter schools are here to stay at least for a few years.

What the members of the board of education seemed to have forgotten was the fact that the charter school must be located in one of the districts it serves, and Willingboro is one of those districts–the largest, in fact. By virtue of the fact that the taxpayers' dollars support both types of schools, it is therefore encumbered upon the Willingboro Board of Education to make every effort to accommo-date the request of the Family Alliance Charter School to grant them space the same as the other districts that the charter school serves. When this did not happen, the Alpha Baptist Church came to the rescue of the charter school by offering one of its buildings to the charter school for a period of one year.

This rather detailed description of a selected action of the Willingboro Board of Education was given because it shows how much time and energy was given to discussion of matters that did not require such at the expense of the children of the district. The Willingboro school district is over 95 percent African-American. Each and every member of the board should never lose sight of that fact and how it got to be that way. Neither should they lose sight of the fact that every day hundreds of children are bused, at taxpayers' expense, out of Willingboro to private schools mainly because the parents of those children do not have the same faith in the public schools of Willingboro that they have in other private schools. Are those other schools better? Are charter schools better? Instead of dealing with those questions, the board of education should be trying to make sure that the public schools of Willingboro are the best. They once were among the very best in the country and they can get to that position again. However, that will not happen until the board of education recognizes the fact that it has to hire a top administrator who they believe is capable of moving this district into the next century, unashamed of its progress and unafraid of the challenges it faces.

The new superintendent, Dorothy Dallah Ph.D., was among the first persons that I interviewed after beginning this story. I had met her before and had been in her presence since, and each time she speaks, her voice rings with high hopes for the district and every student in it. She has a lot of ideas about building bridges between the school, community, home, school board, and faith community. African-Americans, perhaps more than any other ethnic group in America, know the value of cooperative relationships, especially between the home, church, and school. The superintendent recognizes that the time has come for everyone in the community to work together toward what must be a common goal–the best possible education of the African-American children in Willingboro. My only suggestion is that she should be listened to and supported by the board of education, partnered by the community and parents, always challenged to do the job for which she is paid, and evaluated on the basis of her performance. The time has come for the members of the board to call a truce among themselves. They will all end up being winners, and the next crop of board members will have a tough act to follow, all to the good of the students in the system. May it be so!

Willingboro Today

SINCE WILLINGBORO has a council/manager form of government, there is no single voice that speaks, with enforcement authority, for the government or the people, even though the mayor is the titular head of government. For ceremonial purposes, the mayor represents the township and is the person whose signature appears on all proclamations from the council and all official documents. The citizens of Willingboro do not participate in the election of the mayor. The office of mayor is customarily rotated, by vote of council members among themselves on an annual basis.

With the term of mayor being so ephemeral, little can be accomplished during one's tenure in office. For that reason, most of the persons who have served as mayor over the past three decades never saw their pet ideas come to fruition during their tenure. However, nothing prevents a former mayor from trying to continue work on his idea as a member of council, where the real power of government resides. And some have done just that.

The township council meets in public session the second Tuesday of each month. However, it is really in the conference meetings where the deliberations and decisions regarding key issues are made that are subsequently aired in public. The five members of the township council, although elected by the citizens, are really a power elite since they are not directly responsive to the citizenry except at election time. Even then, very little evidence is shown of the influence of the citizenry in a township where the majority of the electorate are members of the Democratic Party. Out of a combination of traditional party loyalty and political apathy, the electorate votes for the persons selected by the Democratic Party power brokers, people who are almost totally unknown to most of them, a fact attested to during the research for this writing. Thus, a seat on the Willingboro Township Council is a very safe seat for a Democrat as far as tenure goes and will remain so under the present circumstances.

This phenomenon is repeated in the county, except in that arena, the balance of power is tilted toward the Republicans. The exceptions to this observation are few and far between. The citizens know about this very lopsided way in which the process works, but in many instances they do not know what to do about it and in others, they are apathetic. Whether it is in the township of Willingboro or the county of Burlington, the power players become an interlocking directorate and run the government, seemingly effectively, but they seldom mention the public except when talking about taxes and tax ratables. It is only when you take a closer look at the administrative and operational aspects of these governments that you are able to gain a better assessment as to whether or not they are truly representative of the people whose tax dollars support them.

Since the mayor and the council are distanced from the public, who then speaks for the public? There is only one person left in this circle of authority, and that is the township manager. Norton Bonaparte has been township manager since January 1995. I interviewed Bonaparte on July 28, 1999, while collecting information for this treatise. That interview is reproduced below in order to allow the reader to gain a broader perspective regarding the question I just raised. Comments in parentheses are my comments.

Dr. Bass: To whom do you report?

Mr. Bonaparte: I report to the mayor and township council.

Dr. Bass: What role, Mr. Bonaparte, do you have in the appointment of members of boards, committees, advisory groups, and related entities?

Mr. Bonaparte: The Local Assistance Board oversees the Human Services Department and particularly the State Local Assistance Program. There are five members on the board; the township manager appoints four. On the Human Relations Commission, which seeks to mediate any issues between neighbors and anything dealing with racial problems within the community there are approximately twelve members. The township council appoints six and the township manager appoints six. The Economic Development Advisory Committee to the township council is also a body that is apprised of twelve members. Four of those are statutory appointments, meaning the mayor, deputy mayor, director of the Willingboro Municipal Utility Authority, and the township manager. Four members are appointed by the council and four members are appointed by the township manager. Those are basically the appointments that the manager makes on various boards and commissions within the township.

Dr. Bass: Regarding the planning board, you do not make appointments for that body?

Mr. Bonaparte: That is correct. The planning board and zoning board are appointed by the council. (These are the boards with the real power that impact the lives of all of the people of the township.)

Dr. Bass: We can observe that finally some real movement is taking place on the old Willingboro Plaza; at least buildings are being torn down. Is there a time frame for the completion of the demolition phase of the plaza redevelopment?

Mr. Bonaparte: Yes, the demolition basically has been completed. The buildings that ought to come down have come down. There's still some rubble that needs to be removed. The buildings that remain are the old Sears building, the old Boscov's building, the old Woolworth building, and the old, what's called the power plant, the triangle building behind the Woolworth building. Developers are seeking the development of tenants for the Sears building, as well as the Boscov building. They have been in conversation with the township to move the library into the old Woolworth building and they have somebody else in mind that they are talking to regarding the old power plant, or the building behind Woolworth.

Now the further development of the site, quite frankly, is going to be market driven, we are very anxiously and very assertively marketing the site. It's a very good economy but until people step up to say they are willing to go on the site we're not in a position where we're going to build something with the hopes that somebody is going to come.

Dr. Bass: Eventually, then, this project will have an impact upon property taxes?

Mr. Bonaparte: It is our hope that this will have a tremendous impact to help lessen the burden on the homeowners in the township.

Dr. Bass: The township now has the old John F. Kennedy High School under its jurisdiction; who will benefit most from that acquisition and how?

Mr. Bonaparte: The residents will benefit the most, and they will benefit in a couple of ways. One, if you were to go over there any afternoon, basically you will find that a lot of it is being utilized. There's classroom space where you have the old chemistry and English classes, but then you have what we call the recreational area–the auditorium, the cafeteria, the gymnasium. There are also an auxiliary gymnasium and the learning resource center of the old library. Those spaces are currently being used by the township's recreation department. We have a senior program where the art classes used to be, where we have up to a hundred seniors from nine in the morning until three or four in the afternoon. We have an arrangement with the County Nutrition Program where we provide food services.

We have the gymnasium, which is used for basketball and other activities, and then the auxiliary gyms where you would find everything from aerobics classes for adults, karate classes for teens or for the young people. We have a varied adolescent program through the recreation department that has everything from a community choir to photography classes. We have a tutoring program where students can come after school and get some tutoring. The Willingboro Rotary Club is putting together some programs for tutoring under Dr. LaRocco. It is our intent for the entire community to benefit.

Now in the second part of that building where the classrooms are currently used we have various tenants. Burlington County College has a presence there. We're very interested in maintaining that presence as the Willingboro campus of the Burlington County Community College. We think it's very important for the residents of Willingboro to have easy access to the higher education services that the college provides.

We're looking for the auditorium to serve as a possible theatre for various groups whether it be the Burlington County College Theatre Group or other traveling theatre groups. They could come in and put on presentations that would be very amenable to the Willingboro residents. With the facility there's just so much potential and we're excited about it.

Dr. Bass: Presently, is the building a tax drain for us as citizens of the community?

Mr. Bonaparte: No, I would not say it's a tax drain any more than the Municipal Complex is a tax drain.

Dr. Bass: In speaking to our superintendent of schools recently, there was a one point that she made that should concern the whole township. She expressed that the greatest concern she had for the children of Willingboro in the public schools was one of security. Safety of citizens in Willingboro comes under your domain. Do you feel that is the uppermost concern, that of security? Let me share with you a recent survey report. I read yesterday that the safest place for kids today is inside the schools and on school grounds, so I was kind of surprised when she said that her greatest concern was security.

Mr. Bonaparte: I think that with the Columbine situation and a number of shootings that have taken place at schools, parents and young people should be very concerned about safety in schools and out of schools. The township council, along with the board of education, put on a seminar a couple of months ago. It focused on what we are respectively doing working together in tandem to provide a safe environment and what resources there are available for children that may have issues. And rather than take those children out in a hostile or violent manner to at least be able to get them some counseling. The township offers counseling and the school district offers counseling. I would like to think that your statement is absolutely true that children are very safe in school. One would think that you are very safe in an airplane; that doesn't mean there are never any airplane crashes. The parents' concerns for the young people in the community, I'm sure, are safety as well as the quality of education and the quality of life in general. Why do people want to live in Willingboro? Why would we want people to state that they are very proud to live in Willingboro? We are a very safe community. We just looked at some crime statistics in the last couple of months and we have a lower crime rate than most of the surrounding areas, including Cherry Hill.

Dr. Bass: I have been quite pleased recently, not just because the *Burlington County Times* doesn't place the African-American crime statistics on the front page, but rather because the statistics seem (to show crime) to be going down in Willingboro. Although there are still many kids who are out there on the street, the statistics are very positive. In that same conversation with the superintendent, she indicated that there are a number of students dropping out of school between the grades of ten and twelve, and that was a situation that was replicated across the United States. She did not have all the explanations for this trend, but my concern was twofold. One, you can't force youngsters to go to school after they reach sixteen, and two, if that many are dropping out, what is there for them? What do we offer as a community to those kids who do choose to drop out of school between the tenth and twelfth grades?

Mr. Bonaparte: Dr. Bass, you've put your finger on what I think is probably one of the scariest statistics, not just for Willingboro, but for the country. In New York City, I think, the dropout rate is 60 percent. Particularly when you are looking at the African-American population, Washington, D.C., Detroit, Chicago, and some of the other major metropolitan areas are extremely high. What we're having is a large number of young people without high school degrees who are going to be competing in an information age. And I use the word "competing" just because there is no way they will be able to compete, and therefore, what are their options going to be? I worked in Michigan and I can tell you back then a person without a high school degree could work at Ford, General Motors, putting bolts on Chevrolets and making a decent living to raise a family. If you want to do that now you better know how to use a computer that puts the bolts on the cars. You don't have those blue collar jobs that you used to that people without adequate education could get. Therefore, I think we are going to have a great labor shortage, perhaps not that we don't have the people, but we won't have the people knowledge- able enough to take on the jobs. This builds up frustration, I think, to add to that the expectation of the quality of life that people get from television, from videos, that they're going to expect certain clothes, certain amenities, cars, but yet without the training to have jobs to afford that. Then I think you will see where people will be (using) their own means to get the money, and then that means the police may be coming by.

Dr. Bass: Willingboro, from its inception, and even now, was never designed as a community that had massive employment opportunities for these residents, so that's nothing new. I raised the question mainly because many of the kids who will be living here will not have a bright economic future in this township, although I don't think that we, as a community, can provide jobs that don't exist. So what do we do?

Mr. Bonaparte: Well, you are absolutely right. Mr. Levitt built it as a residential community, and a lot of the residents worked as far away as New York and Philadelphia, but in terms of the young people the jobs certainly are not going to be in Willingboro.

Dr. Bass: Do you have any feel for the racial composition of the township?

Mr. Bonaparte: The last census, actual census, was done in 1989 and 90 and I think Willingboro has undergone a tremendous transformation in demographics since then, so I would be very reluctant to use those numbers. My guess would be that we're looking at Willingboro being closer to 70 percent African-American and 30 percent non-African-American.

Dr. Bass: I've been here long enough, almost thirty years, to see population shifts in both the school population and the population in the township, in terms of race. From your prospective, is there an explanation of these changes in both areas, the township and the schools?

Mr. Bonaparte: From the township perspective, I think that we went through a birth (from) 1958 through the 70s, when (African-American) people started moving in. At that time it was a predominantly all-white community. I'm talking demographics in terms of racial makeup. We had the lawsuit which allowed blacks to move in, and over time we are seeing a lot of blacks move in as the white residents that were here and enjoyed living here get to a point where they like to retire in a normal capacity, moving to Arizona, California, or

Florida. I think it's not unrealistic to think that when looking at buying a home, residents or non-residents will be primarily African-American that move in to buy the homes that become vacant as people move out.

Dr. Bass: Which means, in essence, that white people may not be returning to the vacant houses that are for sale in this town.

Mr. Bonaparte: That's a question I think will best be answered by a realtor. I would like to think that people see Willingboro as a good housing value regardless of race. I think we both know that people will move into certain areas based upon whom they see there.

Dr. Bass: Willingboro is unquestionably one of the best-maintained towns in the United States. I see this from traveling around the country. Why are we not able to maintain the racial balance in this town? Would that also be contributed perhaps to the public school system here?

Mr. Bonaparte: Those are very good questions you asked, and I hope that you understand that I will be giving you my opinion. I may be wrong, and as I said, it's one person's opinion. I think that we have some characteristics that do not bode well for the township in terms of residents moving in. We predominantly have three, four, and five bedroom homes. People buying a four-bedroom home probably have young children. Their concern about the education of their child may (cause them to) think twice about moving into Willingboro because of the reputation, not because of the actual education their child could get. I think that Willingboro schools do provide a very good education. But there is a reputation that the Willingboro school system is not among the better, so therefore, people that are more able to choose where to live because they have the financial means to may choose not to live in Willingboro because of their concern about the education of their child, and I think that's a community issue.

Dr. Bass: These are questions that I would be looking for your opinion on only. What are some of the areas where improvements are needed?

Mr. Bonaparte: In terms of the quality of life in Willingboro I will share with you what people have told me because I've been out and speaking with different groups. I think one of the key issues within the township of Willingboro is taxes. Because Mr. Levitt built it back in the 50's as a residential community, we do not have a commercial tax base that you would have in a Westhampton, Mt. Holly, Cherry Hill, or Mt. Laurel. Therefore, as normal progression, the cost-of-living increase has been primarily borne by Willingboro, where the tax-base is 94 percent residential.

We do not have a big industrial park that helps to carry the burden; that's why it's so important that township council focus its energies on redevelopment of the Willingboro Town Center, the old Willingboro Plaza. We've had various meetings with the people of the Village Mall because those are really the two places where we can engender some development that can help lessen the burden on the homeowner for the taxes. I would say taxes are number one.

The second one, which you have already alluded to, is reputation of the school system. I think people are very concerned about that. And I think that because of that concern, it's made a difference in who is attracted to Willingboro. And depending upon who's attracted to live in Willingboro determines what kind of community we have, which brings me to the third area that I hear concerns about, and that's the property maintenance. And you are absolutely correct that the property maintenance in Willingboro is far better than most other places in the country. I hear, however, that it's not the same as it was twenty and thirty years ago. There are a couple other factors that I think account for that. The first one is twenty years ago you didn't have houses needing new roofs, new gutters, new siding, because they were relatively new. I think we fool ourselves to think there also isn't a demographics issue. If the people who have the financial resources to choose where to live choose not to live in Willingboro, that depresses the prices of the homes in Willingboro. And therefore, the people who are moving into Willingboro are people, in some cases, who couldn't move someplace else, who couldn't afford someplace else; therefore, when they are buying a home and the roof needs to be repaired or the house needs to be painted, we are finding resistance from a financial prospective. And we are also finding resistance from a sociological perspective–don't tell me my house needs to be painted, I'll paint it when I'm ready to paint it; don't tell me my grass is too high, it looks fine to me, I like the dandelions. So there are some changes taking place demographically but they are changes taking place throughout the country. When a resident that's been here for thirty years says it's not the same as it used to be, I agree with them but show me a place that is.

Dr. Bass: How would you characterize the role of African-Americans in Willingboro, apart from their roles on the established boards and commissions, etc.?

Mr. Bonaparte: I think real vital roles for African-Americans are found in their communities, on their streets, on their blocks, whether it's being part of a crime watch, or whether it's the neighbor association where we all take part in helping each other–and that could be noticing people who don't belong in the community as well as having shared experiences of helping new residents when they come into the community to become acclimated (such as telling them) when to put the trash out or when not to put the trash out. But I think that as Willingboro is a residential area, its strength can be having strong ties at the residential level and not just simply being a collection of houses next to each other, but homes where people interact and care about each other.

Dr. Bass: Over the past ten years there have been at least three efforts to change the form of government in Willingboro, including the present effort. None of these has made it to the public in the form of a referendum. One, do you see any ways that the present government could benefit from a change? If so, how? Secondly, would a change in the Charter be necessary in view of any changes that you may think could or should be made?

Mr. Bonaparte: I believe the current system works very well. Your question is, could it be improved. I think that the way that the Willingboro Township Council interacts is very positive. I think they are looking out for all the residents of Willingboro.

I have been in situations and am familiar with situations where the kind of format that's been proposed by the current group has been in effect, and I see some issues with it. For instance, when you have a situation where individual council persons are elected by a board to represent a particular section. I have seen where they are looking out for that section, which at times could be detrimental to other sections; For instance, when we look right now to see what roads in Willingboro will be repaved, because after a time all the roads wear out. We look to the township engineer to do an engineering assessment. The engineer brings his assessment, saying these are the roads that need to be repaved; this is a priority, this is what we think we should do. And the council accepts that and has the roads done based upon an engineer's assessment. I've seen situations where that information would not be acted upon because it seems as though it was flawed. I'll take Willingboro, let's say the Pennypacker section–if that was the first section built, that may be where more roads may need to be fixed, but to have only roads in Pennypacker done and not Buckingham and not Garfield, the person on the council representing the Garfield section might say, "I'm not going to vote to have only the Pennypacker roads to be done. I need some roads in my section done too because the people that voted for me are going to vote for me only if they see me advocating their interest." So what I've seen in the past is some devoutness, when people are not there to represent the entire community but are there to represent special interests in the community.

The other (argument) that I've heard is that the elected mayor has more clout in Trenton. I've been fortunate to be asked by Governor Whitman to serve on the property tax commission, which was the commission to look at why property taxes are as high as they are in the state of New Jersey, and there were two mayors on that commission, but there were also administrators such as myself and school superintendents. And I could say that from my experience having a separately elected mayor–because we do have a mayor–but to have a separately elected mayor does not give any more weight than the kind of system we have in Willingboro, at least from my experience in Trenton.

Dr. Bass: I think that there are probably as many minds on that particular issue as there are people out there speaking on it. And if I could probe just a little bit further, because I know a lot of people who subscribe to the Thomas Merton view of pattern maintenance–simply stated with some latitude taken, if it ain't broken don't fix it but on the other hand the township council, I am sure from what I know of them, went through a very rigorous process in selecting you as the township manager from among many other candidates. However, the general population of Willingboro does not have as much of an appreciation for your leadership as the township council does because of the form of government that we have. One of the things I say now, and it's probably a little bit biased, is that if we have the best person that could possibly be chosen as our township manager, shouldn't that person have higher visibility than what the office of manager has? You might not want to answer that, but it just makes sense to me.

Mr. Bonaparte: Well, I think the offices of highest visibility should be the mayor and council because the manager reports to and works for the mayor and council under this system. And even when you have an elected mayor you can have a system that you still have a city manager, whether it's the city of Cincinnati or San Diego, they all have mayors and they have city managers, and the managers are responsible, as here, for the day-to-day operations of the government. So are there systems that have a separately elected mayor? Yes. That have also a city manager? Absolutely. The mayor's role is a little different than that of the city manager.

Dr. Bass: What I think, though, Mr. Bonaparte, is that I don't believe that the people of Willingboro fully understand your role, and I think because of that some of them, although they may not support the change of government, some of them are a little bit leery as to what actually happens and how it happens. That's why I raised the question that sometimes that which is good could be improved upon without having a whole charter change.

Mr. Bonaparte: Understood, and if I'm understanding you correctly, more understanding of the office of the manager would be helpful.

I do not know what the reader's response will be regarding the issue of who reports to the public. Frankly, I do not believe that the question can be answered from what was reported in the interview at all. The answer to that perhaps cannot be garnered from any one person or group of persons. For example, prior to this interview with the township manager, I had previously interviewed William Kearns, Esq., the township solicitor, Rabbi Richard Levine, the rabbi who was the spiritual leader of Temple Emanuel Synagogue for over thirty years in Willingboro, a congregation that recently moved from Willingboro to Mt. Laurel; Leonard Mason, code enforcement officer/building inspector; and a few other persons who have been living in the township for fifteen or more years. I refer to them as a control group because as far as I was able to determine all of the respondents in this group were Democrats.

What is most significant about this control group is the fact that without exception, they all believe that Willingboro is an excellent town in which to live and, on balance, it ranks among the best in the state or the country as far as that matters, and they do not believe that there is a need for a change in government. When I talked to Republicans who have lived in Willingboro for fifteen or more years, the picture they painted was not so pretty as that of the Democrats. In an effort to better determine whether or not these varying views regarding the report card of the township reflected true differences in what was perceived or only a reflection of the political persuasion of the respondents, I examined others' aspects of the township structure.

When I obtained and examined the list of all of the boards, committees, commissions, and other statutory groups in Willingboro, I was able to make the following observations.

1. There are fifteen such units in the township, with provisions for 133 members and alternates.

2. Of these fifteen units, the township manager does not make a single appointment to a board with high visibility or one that controls an appreciative piece of the $22,000 budget; this is a function left entirely to the council. This same pattern prevails with the mayoral appointments.

3. All of the appointments to the units that have recognizable power and substantial prestige remain in the domain of the council, which more than likely means that they are patronage appointments.

4. There are several instances where one person has a position on two or more units, and the same phenomenon applies to husbands and wives, as well.

5. There are several occasions where a person has been on the same unit for several years, and others where persons are relatively new to the community but have already staked out a place in the political structure of Willingboro.

Looking at items 3, 4, and 5, one might see that power sharing is driven more by politics than by a genuine effort to recruit members from a cross-section of the community to serve on the various boards, commissions, committees, and other statutory groups. This remains true even when you factor in those statutory appointments for the above units.

While it is true that the township manager wears the headpiece of chief, it is the braves who run the government through the council vis-a-vis the Democratic Party. This becomes very significant as it regards the impact of the African-American in Willingboro. One has to look very hard to find instances where an African-American won a seat on the council without first having been appointed by the council to fill an unexpired term of a white member's vacated seat. As I recall, that is how Marie White Bell gained her seat on council and went on to become the first African-American municipal court judge by the vote of a majority white political structure, and from there she became the first female African-American judge of the Superior Court in Burlington County.

This is not to imply that she was not qualified for these positions or did not work to earn her spurs. To the contrary, Judge Bell was an excellent councilwoman, a truly honorable mayor, a superior municipal judge, and is already winning high marks as a superior court judge. What is really being suggested is that African-Americans have never harnessed their economic, educational, or demographic powers equal to the strength they have in those areas. The African-American population in Willingboro has, since the first family moved into the township, reflected a well-educated and economically stable group. Even when one considers the growing number of lower middle class African-Americans who are residents of Willingboro, that fact alone is not sufficient to alter the power potential of the group at all. Given the fact that African-Americans comprise the majority group in Willingboro (60-70 percent as estimated by many, a figure that may rise by the time of the next census, and more than 95 percent of the public school population), they have substantial political power potential to harness. In effect, the African-Americans provide, by sheer virtue of their numbers, the larger portion of the funds collected from the taxpayers that are raised locally for the support of the budgets for the municipality and the school system. Those numbers would translate into overarching power in all areas of the political spectrum for the African-Americans if they were sufficiently bonded as a group.

Could this be what was meant by the woman who was referenced at the beginning of this account when it was said that African-Americans were not too smart because they did not know the power that they had? If it is, then I must say that those in power have a very clever way of distracting people from the truth.

The power in the township of Willingboro is in the hands of the township council, where three of the five members are African-Americans, and it has been this way for several years. Any lack of full justice in the governmental structure of Willingboro must be laid, first of all, at the feet of those African-American members of council, since they have been in the majority for some time now.

But there is another issue here also, because all of them are not excluded when it comes to members of the same family occupying one or more of the 133 seats on the various units of government. It seems from all appearances that everything is alive and well in Willingboro. Even when I factor in the comments from those persons that I interviewed, I observed some desires for improvement in a few areas of the township but no hue and cry for significant change. However, that must not be construed as meaning that the citizens of Willingboro do not desire a change.

Recently, a group founded by Stanley Fischman called "Citizens for Better Local Government" collected approximately 4,000 signatures to have a referendum placed on the November ballot calling for a change in the present form of government. These citizens are seeking a government that would be more representative of the people, with a mayor elected by the people. Even if some of those signatures are not valid (up to 1,000) and the petition itself is flawed, as has been reported in the press, there is still strong evidence of a grassroots cry for a change in the Willingboro government.

Council could have put the issue on the ballot without a petition but chose not to because they did not see the need for a change. However, if the matter of a change of government is not placed before the people, it may have the same effect that many of those in power felt that a new government would have. More specifically, they felt that a division within the people of the township would occur. If there is going to be a division, history has shown that it is better to let the division come through a democratic process controlled by the electorate rather than by a power elite deliberately withholding the choice from the people. At least, the city would have spoken no matter how small the majority.

Although the Alpha Church hosted meetings for the "Citizens for Better Local Government" when they could not find another suitable place, the church did not take a stand on the issue; nor did I. However, I did conduct a nonscientific sample that might be of interest to the reader. Over a period of two weeks, I asked 150 people (50 from the Kennedy Plaza, 40 from ACME Plaza, 35 from Path Mart in Edgewater Park, and 25 from the Country Club Plaza) the same questions. What are the names of the mayor of Willingboro, the township manager, and the members of the township council? Their responses were as follows: 11 named at least one member of council, five named the township manager, and one respondent named the mayor. The location of this nonscientific sample did not matter because only responses from respondents who lived in Willingboro were tabulated. Although I hope to replicate this sample in the near future, a few additional features of this sample are worth noting. Of the 150 respondents, 141 were adult and 9 were youth, 122 were African-American and 22 were white. There were 127 women and 23 men. It was the white respondents who knew most of the answers to the three questions asked.

I would not want to build a master's thesis on the results of such a sample, but it does seem to suggest that the people in power are not known by the members at the grassroots level. I conducted a small study at the Alpha Complex, which included members of the Alpha Church, parents of children at the day care center, and clients at the beauty salon for a total of 44 respondents, of which 41 were African-Americans. They were asked the same three questions and the results: 13 respondents knew at least one member of council, none knew the mayor and two knew the township manager. There was one change in this sample, which asked the respondents to name the members of the Willingboro school board. Every respondent knew at least one or more members of the school board. Most added an unsolicited comment that let me know that the members were not held in high regard. I did not follow up on that aspect of the survey, however.

If I disregard the results of this nonscientific sampling altogether and just ask myself these three questions, obviously I would be able to name all of the players involved. But the larger question would remain: why? Why is it that I can name all the members of the township council, the mayor, and the township manager? The answer: I have been very active in the community and have had rather sustained exposure to all of them by virtue of my role in the community. If I did not have this role as a pastor, I would probably be responding as did those who participated in my two small studies. The conclusion that I reached from this is that the township may not need or receive a change in the present form of government, but there is a definite need to have a better-informed citizenry. Only when people are accurately informed can they become properly informed. This view is consistent with the township's mission statement, which is quoted below:

> The township of Willingboro is committed to enhancing the quality of life through the delivery of diverse cultural, economic, governmental, and leisure services. It is dedicated to protecting the health, safety, and well-being of its citizens and guests. The Township endeavors to provide a healthy environment in which citizens, both as customers and as those who are the ultimate source of democratic government, as well as employees, are treated with fairness, dignity, and respect. It is the purpose of these goals and objectives to enhance the development and attractiveness of our community to both residents and businesses. The township and its employees will

work in collaboration with its citizens to set the standard for excellence and innovation in the delivery of its services in the most courteous, efficient, and equitable manner possible.

This is an excellent and very aggressive statement, and once translated from paper to action will bring about a more knowledge-able, congenial, and harmonious community, one where the motto, "Where People Care," will become more of a reality. At the same time, mere presentation of this statement suggests a need for change. The offices of the codes official/building inspector, headed by Leonard Mason, already typify the spirit of the mission statement. It is a real pleasure going into that office, although you may be dis-appointed with some of the answers that you receive, the extra requirements that you must meet, the fees that you have to pay, or the notice of the violation that you received. The staff still lessens the pain of this extra burden by the professional, yet friendly, way in which you are treated.

As I bring this effort to a close, I offer the following suggestions for the decision-makers and citizens of Willingboro for the future.

1. There should be a retreat for all of the members of the staff and the various statutory units where the contents of the mission statement are dealt with until they are internalized.

2. All of the township staff should be required to sign a pledge to abide by the tone and tenor of the mission statement, with some kind of consequences to face for evidence of noncompliance.

3. There should be an EEOC officer with some enforcement authority who is not a political appointee.

4. There should be term limits for all members serving on statutory units along with the requirement that no one could serve more than two terms at any given period. This would allow for a wider spread of citizen participation.

5. No one should serve on any unit until they have completed a mandatory training course designed for public service in general and the targeted unit in particular. This training should be built around the township's mission statement.

6. There should be a phase-out of patronage appointments. This practice at the community level is an outrage. Such practice is more tolerable at the state and federal level because the recipients of such positions have sacrificed time, energy, and other resources to help members of their party get elected,

whereas, in Willingboro, no such commitment is made, nor is it necessary. As was stated earlier, Democrats occupy relatively safe seats and should not have to depend on the members of the Democratic Club for directions as to who should get what seats on the various units. This procedure ignores totally the vast number of qualified voters who cast their votes as loyal Democrats but have no voice beyond that vote.

7. All positions on the various statutory units should be advertised and resumes sought. Applicants should then be screened and the selection made from the best-qualified persons while applying the conditions of item number 2 above.

8. The members of council should hold old-fashioned fireside chats with the citizens at regularly scheduled times and places, with an open agenda. At each session an update of current happenings in the community should be provided in oral and printed form. Churches should definitely be included on the list of places to host these fireside chats. It must not be forgotten that Willingboro is increasingly taking on an African-American culture, which may bode well for the politician who does not want anyone looking over his shoulder, but it does little to increase community participation in government. Go where the people are and don't wait for them to come to you which is not the traditional way of the African-American culture unless there is a real crisis-type issue.

9. The role of the township manager should be enlarged and made more visible. The people of the township have a right to know who is in charge of the store, which is not the case at present.

10. Budget hearings should be strategically set in terms of time and place in order to maximize citizen participation.

11. Establish a closer working relationship with the Willingboro Board of Education to the degree that the law allows. Partnering with the school administration in dealing with youth issues will have a stabilizing effect on the tension in that area.

12. The services of individual professionals for the township should be put out to competitive bids. What is going to induce someone to give us a better price for services rendered or superior services if there is no competition for the job? How is the township going to live up to its mission statement if the council is going to keep certain functions behind closed doors where the public cannot have meaningful input?

13. There should be a separate evaluation task force set up for one purpose: to evaluate the performance of the persons who are serving as professionals for the township. One former medical group of an area hospital lost the bid at contract renewal time for a difference in contract bid of $123,000. Had there never been a bidding process, this would not have been an issue. The presence of a difference of opinion on the real significance of $123,000 in the larger picture of an established track record of superior service did not alter the fact that professionals are not usually tenured in such positions as doctors, lawyers, engineers, and, most recently, school superintendents.

14. Willingboro is a first class township "Where People Care," and this should be demonstrated in every way possible such as having a courtesy desk with a people-friendly receptionist greeting every person entering the building and also a place where complaints, compliments, and suggestions can be left with the assurance that they will be read and considered. They could also be part of the agenda at the fireside chats hosted by members of council.

15. It has seemingly been determined by the powers-that-be that the library be relocated to a space at the soon-to-be reconstructed plaza. Is this the best place for the library? Do we need a larger library? What is the per capita use of the present library in terms of books, periodicals, computers, study desks, and other areas? How does this break down by age? If a feasibility study were not conducted to ask these questions, and perhaps some even more pertinent than these, it is not too late. Why not do it?

16. Engage a marketing consulting firm to seek ways to stabilize the community. Recognize that Willingboro is on the road to becoming an African-American community. Whereas this is not something of which to be ashamed, as people should have the right to live where they choose, it should be cause for pause when we know that the white population is not decreasing because of a high mortality.

17. Find creative ways to identify and close down the illegal and, in some instances, dangerous businesses that are operating in homes in the township.

18. I deliberately focused my comments regarding the township on the interview with the township manager because he is the person who is charged with the day-to-day operations of the

municipality. The comments of other persons that I interviewed were woven into either questions I asked him or into some of the other comments that I wrote as I deemed them appropriate. That seemed rather practical. However, there is another source of power in the community that is also trouble-some to the citizens in ways that are more noticeable than the issues of the township. Here, I refer to the public school system of Willingboro and the nine-member board that governs it.

19. Willingboro should consider operating a "house of transient homeless" who live in the Township. A number of people in Willingboro become homeless for varying periods of time. There are also a lot of houses in Willingboro that have too many families living in them. In both instances, these are matters beyond the immediate control of the affected persons. Willingboro should consider addressing this need by buying one or more of the vacated HUD properties and turning them into low-rent housing for low-income persons, or free-rent housing for persons with no income. More specifically, the township should consider operating one or more group homes in lieu of low-income properties in the township. Some of these homeless people in the township are being abused and otherwise taken advantage of by uncaring people whom they have to beg for temporary accommodations. This program could be run through the welfare office of the township without too much cost to the township. The rent charged would go toward the administration of the home and the mortgage payment. Of course, the township would not be receiving the taxes for the property, but it would benefit for the absence of one additional eyesore reflected by a boarded-up house while at the same time helping to serve humanity. I know this works because we have maintained such a home for years that does not provide us one cent in profit but doesn't cost us very much either, and we are making a small contribution for a good cause.

20. Since the color of Willingboro is predominantly black, African-Americans should take the leadership in ending the racial divide and at the same time create a nonpartisan political action committee composed of African-Americans only. White people should be allowed to assist when asked, but not allowed to be members. This is not meant to divide the races, but rather to take the time necessary to inform the African-American voters. Membership could be opened to whites after the PAC is well

established and strong. The main purpose of this committee should be the monitoring of all elected officials and those who are appointed by them and the tasks that they perform. This committee should issue comprehensive and objective annual report cards to the entire community. Every person seeking office should be screened by this committee, and none of its members should run for office while serving on the committee. The political action committee should conduct an ongoing voter registration drive to ensure that all persons, especially African-Americans, are registered to vote and that they do vote. Information meetings should be held at the local churches, the Foster Military Lodge, and in the Township Center to inform the electorate regarding the candidates seeking office. There should be a separate task force within the political action committee that has as its sole purpose the identification of candidates for positions on the school board, township council, and other units of government should the council fail to reach out to the public for candidates. In no instance should candidates bypass this screening committee.

21. The township council, in a joint effort with the Willingboro Board of Education, should hire a consulting firm that will conduct a comprehensive study and perform a complete analysis of the trending patterns of the population to determine what the needs of the community are today and what they will be over the next five, ten, and fifteen years, with the view that the Township will make adjustments accordingly.

22. The township council should cease trying to defeat efforts to change the form of government and use that energy to see how government can be made to work more effectively. If the above suggestions are not acceptable, then hire an independent firm to conduct a survey among the community to see what is the best course for the citizens of Willingboro.

23. The township should, in cooperation with Burlington County College, create a remedial learning center. The purpose of this center should be to provide counsel, guidance, and remedial help to those students who are not college-ready or who may not choose college but a nonacademic track instead. This will accomplish several things. First, it will allow students who need that little extra encouragement and related skills to be able to catch up to and keep up with their classmates once they enter the academic world. Secondly, it will help the students to

develop a greater sense of self-esteem when they can recognize their potential and prepare for reaching it in a non-threatening environment. Thirdly, it will provide a realistic goal toward which the student can strive to achieve as an alternative to a college degree. Students should be able to move from this remedial program into the regular college without having to take additional noncredit course work that is highly embarrassing. The cost of this program should be shared with the county, state, and the local community. Too many students are dropping out of school before they complete the twelfth grade, and others who are graduating are functionally illiterate, with the greater percentage being African-Americans within the Willingboro Township. In the first instance they see no hope; in the second, they have no hope in the job market. This remedial center could help to end that trend and brighten the future for the African-American students and the community.

24. Willingboro should cooperate with New Jersey Transit and the county to help create a transportation system that will enable the young people to get to the places where jobs are located, all of which are not within walking distance.

These are a few suggestions that are offered as a means of stimulating the thinking of my readers who may be taxpayers in Willingboro. These can be amplified, simplified, or ignored. I trust that to do the latter means that an alternative list will be suggested. To simplify them so they will be better understood by the citizens without watering down their potential for creative change is a good thing. However, not to do anything concerning changes in the infra-structure of Willingboro will be at our own peril, as Willingboro is a good community but is positioned to be a great community with the cooperative efforts of the diverse population working together. The African-Americans should take the leadership in making it happen because they have the most to lose if they don't. Besides, they are paying for the largest piece of the pie because of their numbers, while enjoying the smallest piece because of their lack of full participation in the total process of actions that count the most.

The color of Willingboro is black, a fact that cannot and should not be ignored or hidden in shame. Why can't Willingboro become the premier example of how a community changed from white to black and at the same time continues to strive toward reaching its highest potential? Why can't Willingboro become the envy of the rest of the state and nation as a vibrant model of an inclusive community, which just happened to be mostly African-American, in which all of its citizens take pride? It can, if it will.

This effectively closes Part I of this treatise which was written in the early part of 2000.

Part II
Community Survey Implemented

I BEGIN PART II, where I left off in Part I, with the offering of 24 suggestions which grew out of participant observations and personal interaction among the citizens of Willingboro during the spring, 2000. Take a few minutes to review these suggestions before continuing with the reading of Part II which follows.

In my opinion, it is either because the powers-that-be did not find any substance in the 24 suggestions offered or they were simply too busy focusing upon more personal agendas to be bothered and there was no public pressure brought forth to force attention on these issues. Unfortunately, I believe that the latter two instances carried the day for them. This view is supported by a Community Survey that I conducted among the citizens of Willingboro a few months after Part I of this book was published.

The Survey was randomly conducted among 3998 homes in Willingboro's 11 parks or sections. Of that number, 33 houses had for sale signs on the lawns and 11 were boarded up, thus reducing our sample size to 3,954 occupied units. Survey questionnaires tucked inside of plastic door hangers were left at each of the occupied units. In a large number of instances, someone came to the door and accepted the survey questionnaire. If there was a resident working in the yard, this was also seen as another contact delivery. Altogether, 368 surveys were distributed in this manner. In every instance, a self-addressed envelope was included in the plastic door hanger for an easy return but the stamp had to be purchased by the respondent. This helped to ensure me of the genuineness of their interest.

When the period ended for the return of the questionnaires, I was surprised to discover that 1,350 or 34% had been completed and returned. A ten-percent return would have been statistically significant but a 34% return is nothing less than phenomenal. There were 16 statements on the Survey and the respondents were asked to rank each statement with a number from 1 to 5 indicating the extent to which they agreed with each of the statements. A one (1) suggested a strong agreement while a five (5) suggested a strong disagreement. The numbers 2, 3, and 4 suggested simple agreement, no opinion or simple disagreement. There was also a space at the end of the sheet where comments could be written. Each of the statements reflected input gained from talking to people representing a cross-section of the community, both black and white.

The survey instrument with the tabulated responses of the respondents follows:

Willingboro is a unique community, very different from what its founder, Abraham Levitt, intended: a well-planned all-white working class bedroom community divided into 11 parks, each with its own school, swimming pool and play area. There were approximately 11,000 homes designed to fit into every family budget. A major shopping complex was located on Route 130 with convenience stores and smaller shopping areas scattered throughout the community. The creation of two parks, one large enough to accommodate thousands of residents and one smaller for more intimate gatherings. The plan also included one of the finest golf courses in all of South Jersey.

Today, schools are in disarray and the population is mostly African-American; shops are practically non-existent on Route 130 with both malls closed; the environment has changed; and property taxes are high.

The purpose of this survey is to obtain the current attitudes (feelings) of a representative groups of local residents toward the 'State of Willingboro Facing a New Millennium'.

You can greatly assist by rating your responses to the statements on the survey. The value of your rating will be as follows:

(1) Strongly Agree,

(2) Agree,

(3) No opinion,

(4) Disagree,

(5) Strongly Disagree.

Please enter only one number.

As many of you may know, among the four books that I have published within the last few years, the first edition of A Race Divided dealt with the impact of the African-American presence in this post-Levitt community. It is the only authentic study of its kind ever penned about Willingboro. This effort is designed as an attitudinal study that will help to provide an even more comprehensive view of the township.

Following is the survey with the respondent results following each statement.

Please provide your response to the generic questions (statements) below.

Part I

1. Merck-Medo's plan to locate one of its facilities in Willingboro is a good thing.   1006 (1), 322 (2), 12 (3)

2. Of the 800 new jobs promised, most of them should go to local residents.   1301 (1), 49 (2)

3. Building a new library in the new Town Center is a beneficial move.   62 (1), 23 (3), 973 (4), 292 (5)

4. Willingboro is truly a community where people care. 6 (2), 9 (3), 1089 (4), 255 (5)

5. The residents received adequate information regarding the proposed library. 3 (1), 2 (3), 861(4), 485 (5)

6. Business contacts with township officials and workers have been positive. 8 (1), 3 (2), 804 (3), 221 (4), 314 (5)

Part II

7. The failed effort to float a referendum to change the local government was good. 21 (1), 18 (2), 17 (3), 824 (4), 470 (5)

8. All of the members of Council are genuinely concerned about the citizen. 12 (1), 6 (2), 33 (3), 784 (4), 515 (5)

9. Members of Council earn their pay and perks. 12 (3), 982 (4), 336 (5)

10. A strong second party would be good for local politics. 672 (1), 392 (2), 286 (3)

11. More White residents would have remained in the community if the schools had not lost so much of their former appeal. 3 (1), 22 (2), 18 (3), 862 (4), 445 (5)

12. The annual rise in taxes is justified because of the services rendered. 962 (4), 388 (5)

13. The Township Council is too restrictive with information about the town. 762 (1), 284 (2), 68 (3), 236 (4)

14. There are two many churches in Willingboro and the Hispanic church is not needed. 2 (1), 21 (3), 978 (4), 349 (5)

15. The move by the Council to have the Tax Assessor tax as much church property as possible was a good thing. 1 (1), 3 (2), 6 (3), 1121 (4), 238 (5)

16. Separation of Church and state demands that the Township cut no breaks for religious institutions regardless of the good they may be doing. 1112 (4), 238 (5)

17. Other comments *[space was left for comments]*

All but 18 of the respondents made extensive statements in the comment sections of the questionnaire with many of them writing in the margins or on the back side of the questionnaire. After reading all of the comments it was apparent that most of the respondents were emphasizing those area that they had either a strong agreement or strong disagreement with. I will return to this section again but first I want to offer some observations regarding the tabulated responses on the questionnaire.

The overwhelming majority of the respondents, 1345 to be exact, felt that bringing Merck-Medo to Willingboro was a good thing and all 1350 felt that the estimated 800 jobs should go to local residents. This had more to do with the high unemployment rate in the town than with the kind of qualifications that would be needed to fulfill the job requirements for Merck-Medo, as this information was never publicly given. It was learned later that many of the employees would need experience in the pharmaceutical field.

A surprisingly 1266, or 93%, of the respondents felt that the decision to build the New Library in the Town Center was not a beneficial move. This is no doubt related to the fact that only five of the respondents felt that the citizens had been given less than adequate information regarding the entire library project.

If the responses of these respondents are to be taken as truly representative of the whole community, then Willingboro's slogan or motto, "Where People Care," has lost its value. All but six respondents believe that Willingboro is not a place where people care. This is one of the many areas where people wrote comments to further express their concerns regarding selected statements.

When it came to business contacts with the township citizens and members of Council, two things where evident, about half of the respondents had no opinion, whereas, the other half felt that the contact was not sufficient. Ironically, this is one of the key issues that I observed in the first printing of this book and was one of my recommendations that the members of the Council find ways to improve their relationship with the citizens.

Ninety-eight percent, or 1334 of the respondents, seemed to regret that the effort to change the government in Willingboro failed. This should send a message loud and clear to the Council that most of the people do not have the greatest respect for the way this present government is being operated. This correlates exactly with the number of respondents who felt that members of Council were not concerned about the citizens they represent. This posture is also reflected in the fact that they do not believe that the members of Council deserve their pay and perks. This may partially explain why 78% of the respondents felt that the town needed a strong two-party form of government instead of the present structure with Democrats in control without opposition.

Although most of the white people have left the Willingboro Township, 96% of the respondents did not associate the white exodus with the declining school systems in Willingboro. Although there was not opportunity given for such expression. It is properly safe to say that they felt that the white flight had more to do with the high property taxes in Willingboro, which none of the respondents thought were justified.

Only nine respondents felt there were too many churches in town, a position which is at variance with some of the leadership. None of the respondents felt that strict rules regarding the separation of Church and State should be an issue that would cause Council to direct the Tax Collector to seek ways to collect more Taxes from non-profit organizations.

A selected sampling of the 1344 comments from the respondents are given below. Many of the comments did not relate directly to the survey statements but are included in the summary the same as those with related comments when 15 or more respondents made the same or similar comments.

> "Something must be done about the school system or this community will no longer attract families with school age children, black or white, who hold education as an important value. This must be a priority."

> "Willingboro is a dead town and the town Council and the schools killed it. Together they are forcing people from their homes because of the high taxes and the low test scores in all grade levels. Willingboro which was once the best district in the state and nation is now one of the worst and the lowest in the county. Teachers are overpaid but

they obtain these high salaries because they cry the blues and frighten the administration with the possibility of a strike."

"In order for the schools to regain their appeal, children, and black children in particular, must be taught discipline and respect at home first, then in church and school. They must get away from the notion that if you study and are smart, you are "whitey". Or black youth who are "hip" ought to demonstrate their prowess in sports, in dress, smart talk and boy/girl relationships, and not with their brains."

"Fire the Council, school superintendent and mayor, put a freeze on taxes, or you will not have a town. These people who run things are concerned about their image and not about the town."

"It has now become too dangerous to send children to school. You must be part of a gang to survive even inside the buildings."

"I have lived in Willingboro for (ranges from 25-40) years and things are so bad that they cannot get any worse. When you go to Council meetings you see them sitting up there acting like they are listening to your concerns and will even promise to take some corrective actions, but they never do. This refers to the fact that many home are in un-kept conditions. Many of the administrators both in the local government and in the school system are just putting in their time so they can retire with a good pension:."

"Willingboro is a community where whites and blacks can live together. That is what made it so unique. But now, both whites and blacks who can afford it are leaving Willingboro and it will soon become a slum town the same way the school system is".

"These surveys are good. Hope there is an overwhelming response from the people of Willingboro so they decide to take a more proactive role in the community and the schools. We can't trust the people in power to do what is right. Why should they when the community does not speak as one voice?"

"This town does not care enough about its senior citizens who are on fixed income. There should be a way of making the tax burden a little less of a burden for them."

"The Township ordinances should be revised to be more reflective of the current situations in the community. What about a true youth center in Willingboro that will give the youth place to gather and something to do? (This is another suggestion from Part I.)

"White people will leave because they don't want to live in our neighborhood with us. However, we should receive the highest quality of service and respect across the board. Higher taxes doesn't mean better quality of service. We pay more and get less. How come no one shops around for the better quality of service? You need business-minded people who have a good economic background with a love for the people and not self."

"Building a new Library is a waste of money. We have one now that is not used that much by students and the county library is close by, so why not make Willingboro a Branch Library and the county will help to upgrade it if necessary?"

"The most destructive forces in our town have been the out-of-control raising of the Township and school Board taxes practically every year. The people vote down the tax increase with the ballot but the Township increases the taxes without a ballot vote. If normal households operated like the Township runs this town, they would go bankrupt in a few short years."

"People have to realize that everything is not solved by money and we should begin with those in power in the school administration and the Township Council."

"Black people as a race, who make up the majority of the community, should come together and have a collective voice in our community. Instead we have a few white people telling us what to do, while they raise the property taxes to give themselves perks".

"What can we do as a race of people to bring unity among ourselves instead of being a race divided. We know the problem—now let us find a solution and make it happen".

"Willingboro would be a much better community if we did not have a political system that stinks."

I will end these collective quotes with an except from a respondent who attached a lengthy response to the survey questionnaire.

"Being a good resident of Willingboro means more than just living here and paying taxes. Residents need to stop grumbling among themselves and speak up at public meetings where their voices will be heard by those who make decisions that affect our town. An actively involved citizenry would not accept complacency.... Set a good example, be a watchdog, report illegal and/or questionable activities to the Township Manager and the Public Safety Director, Keep up our houses, properties and neighbor-hoods, volunteer.   Regarding question number 16 about the Willingboro School Board renting school space to the Cathedral of Love Christian School at a reduced rate shows illegal favoritism. The question of a reduced rate for one church group and not all church groups is in itself an illegal motion and the fact that the Willingboro School Board has a member who has a relationship with the Cathedral of Love Church and did not recuse himself is a direct conflict of interest and he should not have been allowed to vote. Where was our School Board President and Solicitor when this was allowed to happen? Can we, the public, force a Court ruling on this issue? ....."

Now to bring closure to the direct input from respondents I am going to print a statement sent to me, by my request, from Dr. Robert K. Smith who for many years was the pastor of the St. Paul United Methodist Church of Willingboro. In keeping with my promise, the stated is being included without any edition of content. I think you will find it interesting.

"Change is an expected part of God's created order on earth. Willingboro is changing every year, and whether or not we personally agree with, or approve of change, it is going to happen. Because of some life coincidences, I have been part of Willingboro at two different times, and in two different "generations" (using the theory of sociologist who define a generation as covering twenty-five years.)

"Our family lived in the Buckingham Park section for ten years during the "first generation" of the Township's life. It was a generation when the Levitt concepts of providing public education, recreation, and religious opportunities in as wide-spread a way as possible for the benefit of the residents. This concept greatly assisted with the homogeneity of the town. Families had plenty of opportunities to meet other families. This "town spirit" engendered sports activities for all ages, parades that were a stimulus to unity, and wide-spread caring about the respective parts in which we lived. Events such as block parties were common. Support of public schools, their sports events and other extra-curricular activities, drew participation and interest from our homes. We even learned to live with the reality that our neighbors may move with more frequency than we liked. These moves were largely the result of new assignments for military families, and the belief that if you wanted to move up within our company, it sometimes meant moving on to a new position in another place. At least, this was the experience we had with the parish we were servicing at that time—in ten years we had as many members of the congregation move away as moved into the town and the environs. The one constant in that mobility time was that families sought religious affiliations as part of settling into their new community. During this first "generation" of the Township's new suburban status, there were well-supported inter-church events which aided in keeping the sense of community alive and well. There were factors that began to occur toward the latter part of this first "generation" in town: the military did not make transfers as frequently, more of those in the military were able to retire in town, corporations found the costs of moving personnel too high and so reduced their moves, and as families became affluent they chose to relocate to larger homes in other parts of the county. One result was a gradual change in the ethnic composition of the Township, with homes once owned by Caucasians being acquired by African-Americans, Latinos, and Asians.

"The present or "second generation" of life in Willingboro reveals that the Caucasian population is now minority to the sum total of the other residents. Another major reality is that considerable numbers of "first generation" home-owners paid their mortgages, had their children mature and move outside the Township into their own education, careers, and home in other places. The number of school-aged children has diminished, requiring

fewer public education and recreational facilities. The
religious preferences of those now in the community has led
to some substantial changes in types of congregations. For
instance, the Jewish religious community is so small that
both of the previous synagogues have relocated outside the
Township. The churches often collectively referred to as
"the main-line Protestant Churches," such as Episcopalian,
the Lutheran, the United Methodist, the Presbyterian, and
the Reformed, have witnessed reductions in church
membership—even though all of them were and are multi-
racial in congregational make-up. The Roman Catholic
Church continues to be a strong congregation, although
smaller than at some earlier times. The Baptist Churches
have grown in number, as have independent congregations,
with larger or entirely non-Caucasian memberships. These
newer churches are attracting persons through the styles of
worship, fellowship, music, and support being offered to
those affiliated with them. The spiritual vitality is just as
vibrant as it has ever been, but it is being satisfied in the
ways that meet the spiritual needs and interest of those who
comprise the respective congregations.

"The cooperative spirit among these churches experienced
a waning for a period of time covering the end of the "first
generation" and the commencing of the "second generation."
Part of the reason is that some of the early history was not
carried over by the churches and their sense of cooperation
for the benefit of the religious community and the Township.
In recent years, persons such as Dr. Joseph O. Bass, and some
others who remain aware of the great good that has been
accomplished when the religious community works together,
have re-awakened an ecumenical and cooperative spirit. The
community welcomes this presence, and especially welcomes
the good influence which the co-operating religious
community can bring to Willingboro, for the benefit of the
residents. The community paid a noticeable price during the
vacuum of the religious voice and presence. The obvious
conclusion is that the original ideas of the Levitt planning, to
have religious institutions present throughout Willingboro, is
for the personal and the corporation benefit of the people.
Now, in the latter years of Willingboro's "second generation of
history," with so many of the original residents no longer on
this side of eternity, it is up to the collective wisdom of the

religious community, in concert, in cooperation, and continually in their dialogue, to pray to know the good will of God; and to be the messengers to keep it spoken and effective for the Township. The poet Edward Everett Hale writes;

"I am only one,
    But still I am one.
I cannot do everything,
    But still I can do something:
And because I cannot do everything
    I will not refuse to do the something that I can do."

Rev. Dr. Robert K. Symth, Co-Pastor

Holy Trinity United Church of Christ

July 17, 2000

It is quite apparent from these responses to the survey statements and the added comments that Willingboro was still in a crisis mode as late as mid-2000. However, Dr, Symth seems to express it different- ly by saying that Willingboro was a changed community which has the potential for crisis but also the potential for unprecedented positive growth.

But those opinions along with Part I of this book represented a Willingboro up to the end of Century 2000. Change is ubiquitous and Willingboro has undergone a lot of changes during the past three years which I will briefly examine.

Changes in Willingboro

Most of the changes that have taken place in Willingboro have occurred during the past year or so and I will mention them and you be the judge as to whether or not they were positive.

There have been a few changes in the infrastructure of Willing- boro especially as it relates to the Township Council and positions under their control.

William Kearns, who had been the Township Solicitor, for more years than even I can remember, was suddenly removed from office by the five-member Township Council, whose membership is now three blacks and two whites. The vote was three to two for removal along color lines. There was a cry of racism by one white member on the Council which was without real evidence. In fact, I wrote a letter to the Editor of the *Burlington County Times,* and to Council, defending the action as being more political than racial but equally wrong. To me it was clear exercise of newly-acquired political clout by the black majority on Council. Kearns himself chose to take the decision in stride, although he first learned that the change was to take place from a reporter who had advance information of the pending action.

The black members of council held that they were taking the action ahead of Kearns' alleged resignation, which was to occur on his 65th birthday–something that Kearns himself denies. He was replaced with Michael Armstrong, a young, bright and well-known local criminal attorney who has had a long-standing association with the judicial system of Willingboro and who is also employed by the Council part-time in the legal field. Although soft-spoken, he is very intelligent, honest and a respected attorney who will be objective in his opinions to Council but will probably never have the political clout that Kearns wielded. Almost everything that happened at the Council level, and with politics in general in Willingboro, showed some signs of Kearns' involvement. Kearns still maintains his law firm in Willingboro, although he is less visible than before, but there is no hard evidence that he is completely working behind the scene.

For reasons again that were strictly political, there are now separate Engineers for the Planning Board and the Township proper. This creates extra costs for the applicant seeking site approvals for construction in the Township, not to mention the fact of the extra burden of having to deal with two professionals, instead of one, for the same job. It is no accident that these two Engineers assigned to Willingboro by the white firms, for which they work, are black. This move was entirely unnecessary and has not set well with everyone – not even the people who made the decision.

Most of the conflict seems to revolve around the Township Engineer who sees himself as not only the one who must sign off on every project before a Certificate of Occupancy can be issued, but also as a little god whose duty it is to protect the Township even from non-existing dangers. He has been accused of abusing his power and overcharging for inspections of work done in the Township. More than once, he has been reported to the State professional Board that governs Engineers in the state, only to have the cases withdrawn later out of a desire to avoid a racial confrontation. But this man does not ever admit to any mistake that he has made, nor does he restrict his involvement to the relevant issue of the case before the Planning Board where the voice of the other black attorney should have equal weight. He always searches for ways to make it appear that he is looking out for the Township. This is basically the result of an insecure black who is the first to hold such a position.

Here is a classic example of the abuse of his powers. A preliminary site plan was approved for a construction project to be erected on a site which called for the removal of a fenced-in playground area. However, by the time the final site plan was approved, the playground had already been moved to a location away from the site and erected elsewhere, in accordance with the properly-issued permits by the office of the Building Inspector. The entire project cost $400.00. The Planning Board Engineer had no problem with this and simply crossed it off the site plan since it was no longer a part of the proposed project. However, Carl Turner, the Township Engineer, instead of accepting a letter stating that the playground had been properly relocated, insisted that it had to be treated as if it were still there. He first said to move it back to the position where it was shown on the site plan, which would have been both ridiculous and impossible as that space was now taken up by an extension to the new building which was already completed.

In spite of the fact that the playground was now in a new location in accordance with guidelines set by the local statues and only cost $400 to construct, Carl Turner still applied a value of $20,000 for bonding purposes for the non-existing playground, as far as the site plan goes, and added the maintenance bond and his inspection fees accordingly, The latter action made it even more unethical since there was no playground for him to inspect and the bond has to remain with the Township for two years when there should not have been a bond at all because no playground was even required by the Township or State department of Human Services. Stubbornly, he has held fast to his ridiculous position, which is supported by the Township Manager and shows what little power she has and how unprofessionally it is used.

The Building Inspector has tried to talk to Carl Turner about the matter, explaining that his office had issued the proper permit for the fence and that it was outside of his jurisdiction. But this has been to no avail.

For those people who know the details of this matter, they say that Carl Turner either does not like the Entity that owns the playground or he is flexing his muscles. To me, it is theft, as well as unethical. Theft because it is taking money that does not belong to the Township, and unethical because he is unwilling to make a simple adjustment to the site plan although a letter has been written saying that the fence is no longer a part of the site under his jurisdiction.

The last word on this is not in yet but this provides the flavor of the kind of insensitive people now in power.

The same Engineer approved a Certificate of Occupancy for the Funeral Home rather arbitrarily. First, he suggested that the funeral home get permission to use the Performance Bond posted by Another Program, which was unethical because the amount was not sufficient to cover two sites. As if this was not unprofessional enough, he authorized the issuing of a Certificate of Occupancy for the funeral home without requiring that a Maintenance Board be posted with the Township. His excuse: He forgot it. This hardly seems possible with one who is the unofficial watchdog for the Township. How can he go back and correct this situation at this late date? Such selective memory fits well with his arbitrary use of his powers, but adds greatly to the racial divide in the Township, since all of the affected parties are black.

The Township manager, was promoted from assistant manager to the top position, after the office was vacated by a gentleman who had grown weary in the job and accepted a similar position in Camden, NJ, which is the most troubled city in the state. The move was understandable because the Willingboro Township Manager has no real power. As an employer of Council, the person simply parrots what the Council dictates and this bodes well for this present council.

Another illustration of the juvenile way in which the Township is often managed is the case where two sisters initiated a joint venture to start two separate businesses in a vacant building which they purchased together. One-half of the building was to be a beauty salon and the other half, an ethnic restaurant. Initially, exterior plans and some interior plans proceeded as though the two business would be allowed to co-exist, although there was only one site plan submitted to the Zoning Board for approval. It was for the beauty shop and was granted. The beauty salon opened, and then the second application was submitted for the restaurant to be located on the other half of the building. The Zoning Board rejected it unconditionally. But the applicant went forward with the idea that the Zoning Board was going to have a change of heart. Work on the site plan was adjusted, traffic studies conducted, parking lot enlarged, firewall built to divide the two entities. Finally, another appearance was made before the Zoning Board. Again the application was rejected in the presence of a large number of supporters from the applicant's church, many of whom spoke in her behalf. The position of the Zoning Board was that the site was not suited for dual usage and such usage had never been requested. It was further stated that granting the original variance was done reluctantly as the site did not meet all of the requirements for a beauty salon. The argument of the applicant was that she had spent $40,000.00 in preparation for this restaurant and had followed all of the verbal advice given to her by people within the township, leading her to believe that the second project would be accepted.

This is a clear case where the need is there for Township officials to put their comments in writing, to citizens who are seeking to build in Willingboro, so as to avoid the kind of unfriendly and unnecessary confrontation which took place at that meeting. It seems as though this is a dead issue now unless the applicant seeks an alternative business for the site where its fate is uncertain if pursued.

There are other cases that can be highlighted to demonstrate the need for a more business-like atmosphere on the part of the people in power. When white people were in power, it could be called racism when things did not work out for the affected parties' satisfaction. Now, with blacks in power in all key positions, this escape technique cannot be applied. Black people must come together and stop trying to flex their muscles and get on with the business of managing the affairs of the Township responsibly. Failure to take this suggestion seriously will result in an even more racially-divided community. The majority of players in these two episodes were black, thus it appears more like a black-on-black issue, which should not have been the case at all.

As one person put it succinctly, Black people are simply not ready. His meaning was that they are not capable of taking care of business in a manner that shows integrity about ego. Nepotism is still prevalent in Council appointments the same as when whites were in power, and perhaps even worse.

No vacancies on Boards and Committees are announced, at least not publicly, no resumes are requested for would-be volunteers on the various Boards, Advisory Counsels and Committees. The same people who have been serving are still serving unless they have been removed by death or have played musical chairs. Even the mayor made the unusual request that he be reappointed for a second consecutive term, as there were things that he wanted to complete during his administration as mayor.

It does not really matter because what the black members want they get because they control the majority of the seats and the office of mayor is a position that, before this instance, had been an annual rotating basis among the members of council. This is not being done in violation of any law; it just a playing into the ego needs of the people in power whereas the real people in need, the citizens, are being ignored.

Just recently, it has come to light that an effort is underway to change the form of government so the mayor can become an elected official. Seemingly, there is a desire to have more power over the entire workforce of the Township. This would effectively do away with the office of the Township manager. Of course this would have to be put before the citizens for a vote. Whereas the respondents of the survey taken in 2000 felt that a change in government might be a good thing, it is not known for sure if this opinion will hold if it is known that the effort is to give more power to the office of the mayor. In short, the struggle goes on inside the hallowed chambers of a select few where the township, as a whole, suffers from the absence of good leadership. It seems that a similar situation prevailed in Gary, Indiana which has never fully recovered.

Before bringing this part to a close, I want to mention a few other changes.

The Library has moved to its new location in the Town Center and was recently opened. Only time will tell if the respondents were correct in their assessment that it was not a good move. One thing is certain: it encountered a large cost overrun which even the Township Council admits. To that degree, the respondent cannot be proven wrong.

Burlington County College has also relocated in the Town Center. Both of these buildings are set back quite a way from Route 130 and their beauty, such as it is, is hardly seen. Merck-Medo has completed its building but its rear is facing Rt. 130 while the front is hardly seen at all from any direction. It added some new jobs and tax revenue, but did nothing for the scenery along Rt. 130. Two banks, Commerce and Farmers and Mechanics along with Burger King are the newest visible entities along 130, which is a little help but not enough to make a passing car slow down a bit so the driver can take a look at how things have changed for the better. The old Sears Building still stands waiting for a buyer. There is talk in the air regarding the building of a high-rise luxurious apartment complex in the Town Center area. Although the voters, a year ago, gave the Township the right to issue a liquor license to an eating establishment that would seat 150 persons, there is no indication that there are applicants lining up to take advantage of this new development. Before the vote, which had failed in every prior attempt, the citizens were told that a number of Restaurants would be interested in acquiring licenses. Where are they? This Council would do well to hire a professional marketing firm to help identify firms that may be persuaded to locate in Willingboro. The latest thing is the possible relocation of the retail Mark in Willingboro. There is a divided opinion on this, as well. The outspoken citizens and members of Council say they want something more upscale than what is represented in the stores that are located in the present Mark that is seeking to relocate. Time will tell who wins out on this one, as it will most likely not be presented to the citizens for a vote; not only because it is not required, but also because the members of Council want the prestige that goes with the decision.

There simply is no space left to write further on the present crisis in Willingboro, but a word must be added regarding the school crisis in the Township. We have another Superintendent of Education. This person is a non-educator and does not hold a doctorate, but he seems to have some good ideas regarding the future course that the educational system should take. Immediately, the problem of textbook shortage, overcrowded classes, school violence and test scores must be tackled. Since Superintendents are no longer given tenure, maybe something good will come from this one. As one pessimistic citizen put it, we are in the pits educationally, and there is no way for us to go but up, and just maybe, Alonzo Kittrels is the man to take us out of the pits. Should this happen, it would also be a challenge to the Township Council. At least we can hope.

Or can we? Looking at the nature of an unethical situation carried out by the Superintendent and one proposed by the two-term mayor cast a shadow on just how ethical they really are and, as well, on how egocentric they can be. More specifically, the State introduced a special program for four-year-old kids living in academically weak school districts (Abbott Districts), to attend public school for a half-day in order to increase their readiness for Kindergarten. The targeted districts could house these kids in their own facilities or farm them out to private providers, as long as the standards were met. The Superintendent of the Willingboro district did not feel that the district was ready to handle the program and would need a year or more to get ready. Therefore the decision was made to farm the program out to various providers. This seemed to have worked fairly well during the first year of the program, but it is hard to tell since there was no evaluation made of any of the contracted providers.

However, for the second year, the Superintendent made the decision that the contract for all of the four-year-old kids would be awarded to the Burlington County Coalition of Child Care Providers (BCCCCP). It was never revealed how the decision was reached to eliminate the other providers and give an exclusive contract to the BCCCCP. Not only that, the BCCCCP, as an entity, had no track record with four-year-old kids since they did not participate as a contracted provider in the first year.

In additional to that dilemma, there was an inner struggle raging among the three Day Care Centers that made up the Coalition of Child Care Providers. (Primary Colors, Different and Wonderful and Alpha Child Care and Developmental Center.) The Alpha Child Care and Developmental Center had always maintained very high standards and was in full compliance with the state and the local district. However, there was a constant battle raging among Alpha and the other two providers over how much profit could be made from the program. Alpha's position was that being a non-profit corporation, it could not take a profit from the program and put it into the pockets of the management teams; whereas, the other two providers were for-profit. Alpha was in the program for the benefit of the children and not for the money, which was a top priority for the other two centers. The other two directors would meet and talk among themselves and, when they came to a Coalition meeting, they had already decided how things would go and that is the way they went because they had the votes.

Finally, Alpha decided to withdraw from the Coalition and advised the Superintendent of its decisions. The remaining members of the Coalition advised the Superintendent that they would take the kids that were at Alpha. Alpha further informed the Superintendent that the kids at its centers were happy there. They had a certified staff who would let them remain in the program at Alpha, at no cost to the parents or district. Alpha said that they would rather bear the brunt of the extra expense for housing the kids, rather than see them uprooted or placed in an inferior program, either with the Coalition or a makeshift one suddenly created by the district.Alpha was content to live with that decision.

Bowing to pressure from the Coalition, the Superintendent, asked Alpha to keep the children and let the district pay for half of them and give the other half of the funds due Alpha to the Coalition. Dr. Bass, the president of the Alpha Community Outreach Program, which runs the Alpha Child Care and Development Center told the Superintendent that what he was proposing was highly unethical but, since his center was determined not to interrupt the educational process of the Children, the suggestion would be reluctantly accepted. So a new contract was drawn up, showing that Alpha had 30 four-year-old kids and was being paid for only fifteen. However, what was not pointed out was the fact that the Coalition was being paid for fifteen of the kids at Alpha, although they never rendered any service to them. This unethical practice continued to the end of the school year when the district took over the program. This offer to give a flavor of the kind of politics that goes on in the Willingboro School district and such little regards for the wise use of the Taxpayers money without any pain or regret for unethical behavior. However, this is the man that everyone is counting on to bring the Willingboro School district from the pits to the point of excellence once again. It if happens, it is hoped that it will be on much higher ethical standards than were applied when trying to solve the dilemma just described.

Regarding the unethical practice on the part of the Mayor of Willingboro, he is a user and does his best to prevent the taxpayers from thinking about the implications of his actions by focusing on what he suggests as a positive. It has already been mentioned that he persuaded the minority members of Council to re-elect him as mayor for a second term, which is not a big deal as that office is more ceremonial than it is vested with power. However, he failed to mention his hidden agenda. He wants to be elected by the people as mayor with full and complete power of the entire township and do away with the office Township manager. In order to accomplish this, a new form of government will have to be voted into law. This requires a referendum from the citizens.

Whereas, the earlier study that I conducted indicated that a change in the governmental structure is needed, it did not focus on the office of mayor. Recently there was a $300.00 per person fund-raiser, spearheaded by the Mayor, to raise funds for his campaign. This is unethical because he wanted to be mayor for the second term so he would be in public view when the referendum was floated.

Like all the other elections that are held in the township, the Democrats shell out a lot of "street money": (money for campaign worker to help garner the votes). The mayor hopes to put this over on the citizens under the guise that the time has come for change in the form of government, when in reality, the time has come in his mind for him to be the godfather of the Township. He has also let it be known that he would give up his current job as principal of an elementary school in Camden. If he can keep blinders on the citizens with his rhetoric and prevent them from doing independent thinking, he just might pull it off. Who knows, worse things could happen at a time when the race is as divided as it is in Willingboro.

I do need to mention the fact that in the Willingboro infra-
structure, there are two offices that are outside of the loop when it
comes to being a negative factor in the positive influence of African
Americans in the Township. One is the office of the Township
Clerk. There are three people in that office, two of whom deal
directly with the public, the Township Clerk and the Deputy
Township Clerk, while the third worker just speaks and smiles at
the people who come and go, while she works quietly at her computer. Although they are long time employees of the Township they
are both in recently move-up successor positions as the Clerk and
deputy respectively. What is so unique about these two ladies is
the positive attitude that they maintain when dealing with all sorts
of citizens, many of whom show attitudes from frustration to outrage
because they have come to that office to pay their fees. Many of
them often fuss and grumble, whether paying a small sum for dog,
cat or bicycle license, or a huge fee for a Performance Bond for a
major construction job. I have known these extraordinary ladies for
many years and have dealt when them personally, dozens of times,
and have never seen them treat any citizen with anything less than
true professionalism and the ultimate respect. On many occasions
they will take extra time to explain the fee structures and the reasons
for the same in order that the citizens may leave in a better spirit
than when they came. That office is a big plus for the Township of
Willingboro.

Then there is the office of the Building Inspector. This office
has many functions and an efficient staff to attend to each of them,
including issuing of all permits for all building projects, residential
and corporate, as well as subsequent changes or additions to these
structures. This includes something as simple as issuing a permit to
erect a fence between properties to something as complex as
multiple permits for the new library or the Willingboro campus of
Burlington County College. It oversees the inspection of all of the
11,000 residential units in the township to ensure that they are kept
up to code, both on the interior (required at time of rental or sale of
a property) and the exterior of all properties, on an ongoing basis.

The fire Marshall works out of this office as well as the
plumbing, heating and electrical inspectors. Perhaps as many
people come to the office to complain about something as come to
get permits. They especially become annoyed when they have
failed to obtain permission from the Planning or Zoning Boards to
move forward on a project for which they have already spent large
sums of money. Leonard Mason, who is the Director of the entire

department, has to take the anguish from many irate citizens who are really angry with someone else or another entity in the Township Council-controlled system. However, since it is hard to reach the members of Council, they do what they consider the next best thing, take it out on staff in Mason's office. In spite of all the negative comments hurled at the staff in the office of the Building Inspector, Mason and his requisite support staff show kindness and offer sound advice, even in areas where they do not have a direct responsibility. They do it in order to help Willingboro live up to its motto, "where people care". If all people connected with the governance of the Township were as citizen- and student-focused as the staff in these two offices, then Willingboro would not have a problem in either the schools or the Township. In fact, it would be, in every sense, a residential community even greater than its racist founder, Abraham Levitt, envisioned. Although all of the power is basically in the hands of the African-Americans, unfortunately, it is not being used any more productively that it is in other places where the power held by African-Americans is real but not as great.

Summary

Willingboro has emerged as a middle class community, almost completely replacing the white inhabitants, who once comprised 100% of the population and today make up less than fifteen percent of the total population, although this is not shown by any census data. In reality, the white population may be less or more, depending upon whom you ask. However, it is certain that the public school enrollment is less than one percent white. What is left is a population of African-Americans, Hispanic, Asians and Puerto Ricans, with Blacks comprising over 90 percent and the other ethnic groups sharing a combined nine percent. The black population, by their sheer number, are in control of the politics, fraternal organizations, economic and educational structures, social arenas and religious institutions. The only exception is the Willingboro Rotary Club, with 55 members, approximately two-thirds of whom are white and mostly senior citizens. Many of them do not live in Willingboro, but have maintained their membership in the Willingboro Club, primarily for business and friendship reasons.

Now we come to the conclusion of the treatise on Willingboro. In a number of ways, it is very sad. First, we have to acknowledge that there are no identifiable African-Americans leaders in Willingboro, no one with the prestige and influence to give direction and guidance in any arena to this new community of Black people. Secondly, there is an absence of any fraternal organization that can assume the role of leadership. Third, at one time, the Willingboro Clergy Association, was a strong coalition for justice, but not anymore. The Willingboro NAACP is no longer in a position of influence and its membership is down to two-digit numbers, as far as active members go. The newer groups, such as Afri-Female and Afri-Male (now Boys and Girls Clubs), are without influence.

In short, there is no collective voice which can speak for Willingboro today. Unfortunately, this applies to the historical African-American church, which has traditionally been the voice of the Black community. There are more of them today, but each one is going its separate way, with no signs of coming together as a cohesive force for good. In fact, one of the saddest stories, happening in Willingboro today, regards the entire concept of the racial divide and ethnic in-fighting among the religious houses of worship. In one instance, one congregation purchased a building from the Jews, who had vacated it when the congregants moved out of the community. It was not very long before there was a fight among the new inhabitants. Consequently, the chief executive of the denomination had to be summoned to attempt to settle the dispute. Having no success, the matter went to court, where it was settled by a judge, but left a negative impact upon the two group, in particular, and the community in general.

In two other instances, two ministers, who were members of different congregations, left their respective churches, taking with them enough members to start new congregations.

Perhaps the most notorious example of a church losing its touch with the mandate given to it by Scripture is the Alpha Baptist Church. During the first twenty-five years of its history, the Alpha Baptist Church was the leading church in Willingboro . It was in the forefront of the fight for righteousness and justice for everyone, with a stellar reputation that was known and respected throughout the community, county and beyond. This was due both to its dynamic leader who had a national and international reputation and the loyal, caring and informed following. This church was a part of every good cause that presented itself and it often led in the fight for justice, without the aid and assistance of others who simply benefitted from its leadership.

However, this all came to a halt when the founder resigned after twenty-five years and become the pastor emeritus. He personally selected his successor, an individual whom he had previously licensed to the ministry and designated as his successor years earlier. What happened after his son in the ministry was installed is difficult to believe and painful to relate. Within a period of four days, this new pastor had turned on his father in the ministry and began a campaign to destroy his reputation by all means necessary and possible. He removed all of the members of the leadership team, Deacons and trustees, whom he felt he could not control, and replaced them with people he could control. This included all of the trustees, except one whom he could turn into a "yes man," and the women on the Deacon Board, in addition to some other leaders. As if this were not enough to damage the reputation of the former pastor, he would spend Sunday after Sunday talking negatively about the church which existed before his arrival.

This was followed by a legal action taken against the former pastor, which was baseless; but, he was pastor and, as such, had made himself a little God. The action involved a Resolution that had been officially passed by the Trustees and Deacons and which recognized the land and buildings across from the church as belonging to the former pastor, because he had purchased the land and erected the buildings. Although the church had no financial interest in the property whatever, the devil-driven pastor took advantage of the fact that the original pastor had made the purchases while he was serving as the pastor of the Alpha Church and, therefore, assumed it gave the church claim to the buildings and the land.

Of course, once this matter goes to trial, his opinion will be replaced with factual evidence. In the meantime, he has prevented the church from paying the pastor several hundred thousands of dollars due him for salary deferred, withheld salary and loans made to the church. Even the gesture made by the former pastor to forego half of what was owed him, if the church would do the right thing and support the resolution, was turned down by the new pastor. He has been able to get his accepted and handpicked leaders to tell many lies, concerning the former pastor, in his efforts to totally demonize him. This man is so bold that he performs weddings without being ordained, which is illegal. He has taken a handi-capped parking place and changed it to his own private parking place, so he is now able to park nearer to the entrance of the church. Almost everything the church was doing for the good of the members and the community, he has discontinued.

To add fuel to the flame, he gave an interview, which contained more than a few lies, to a reporter of the Leading Newspaper of the county. For example, he said there were only 40 members of the church when he became pastor, when in effect there were more than 40 members in the choirs alone. He implied there were no choirs when he came, but there were actually five functioning choirs, which he now takes credit for. He said there was no Bible Study, when in reality there was, with the adult class being so large that they were seeking newer space. He claims that the finances were in disarray and almost non-existent when, in fact, the church was operating on a budget of nearly $200,000.00 and had no outstanding bills, except what was owed to the former pastor and a mortgage on the real property, which was current. Additionally, there was $40,000.00 in the bank. These are only a few of the lies that he told. No one knows the motives behind his assault on the reputation of the pastor. But one thing is for sure, Truth crushed to the earth will rise again. When this matter is litigated by the court and a jury, this man, who apparently is inspired by Satan, will lose.

But, in the interim, the church which thinks it is being led by a man of God is suffering and will suffer more. Not only that, but Willingboro's last and best hope is gone. Now, it is up to the Lord. Will He divinely intervene or inspire some new leadership? That is in the future and time will tell. It is doubtful that another book will be written on Willingboro, so there are only two ways of knowing how this racially divided community will fare in the future. One, look for something in the media as this is a huge story or, two, check out the Alpha website. http://www.alpha-intl.org.

Walking with God

I go walking alone with God at my side,

I chose to walk alone with him by faith

than walk by myself in the light

enduring the walk until I reach heaven's gate.

JOSEPH O. BASS

About the Author

The life of Dr. Joseph O. Bass has been marked by great adversity, as well as extraordinary achievement. The unexplained death of his father, the subsequent loss of the family farm in Mississippi, the unwavering faith of his mother who worked tirelessly to raise her eight children, and his deportment from Mississippi, all acquainted the author with the best and worst of the human spirit at an early age. Dr. Bass overcame ethnic and social barriers to become a successful pastor, industrial missionary and noted scholar of religion, ethics, history and sociology. This remarkable spiritual leader is the founder of the Alpha Baptist Church of Christ, the Alpha Complex - a minority Economic Development Enterprise, the Alpha International Academy of Excellence, The Alpha Community Outreach Program and the Alpha Ethical Society. He was the first African- American to become a member of the Rotary International Club in Thailand and the first African-American to have an audience with His Majesty, the King of Thailand. Because of Dr. Bass' unique role in effecting positive change in the Thai society, he was personally requested by the American Ambassador to deliver the message to the International Community at a special Memorial Service honoring the death of Dr. Martin Luther King, Jr. The author's life experiences are described in vivid detail in his powerfully moving biographical work entitled *Without Vengeance* and published in 1999, 2002, and 2003.

www.ingramcontent.com/pod-product-compliance
Lightning Source LLC
Chambersburg PA
CBHW020417290526
45785CB00002B/611